ZERO WASTE ECONOMY

Christian Heritage Rediscovered

The Series, as the name suggests, is meant to focus on Christian Faith & Living vis-à-vis topics like Literature & Poetry, Indigenous Philosophizing, Ethical response towards Agriculture, Health & Healing, Science & Technology, Eco-feminist Theology, Sociological approach towards Human Rights, Law & Politics, Arts, History of Ideas, Ancient Civilizations, Cultural Contiguity, Religious Cosmologies & Mysticism, Footsteps of famous Theologians, World Peace & Harmony, Global Capitalism, Network Marketing, Cybertheology, Population & Demographics, Epigraphic Studies, Contextualized Education, and many others. We welcome a Mss. on any topic/s mentioned, whether they are original works, scholarly monographs, collections of conference papers, revised dissertations, or translations of historical documents. Through the Series we, the Publishers, are striving to put forward published works that may help Institutions, Academic Bodies, Researchers, Scholars and the World at large in furthering their respective knowledge and understanding on the concerned subject. We welcome your comments on our efforts and further suggestions on how we can foster the upcoming thought provoking theologically grounded books.

Christian Heritage Rediscovered - 42

ZERO WASTE ECONOMY

Theological Insights for Urban Sustainable Waste Management

R. Shibu Mayam

CWI
Christian World Imprints™

First Published in 2016 by

Christian World Imprints™
Christian Publishing & Books from India
H-12 Bali Nagar, **New Delhi-110015**
info@christianworldimprints.com
www.ChristianWorldImprints.com
Phone: +91 11 25465925

ISBN: 978-93-5148-145-4 (HB) ISBN: 978-93-5148-146-1 (PB)

Cataloging in Publication Data--DK
Courtesy: D.K. Agencies (P) Ltd. <docinfo@dkagencies.com>

Shibu Mayam, R., 1981- **author.**
Zero waste economy : theological insights for urban sustainable waste management / R. Shibu Mayam.
pages cm. -- (Christian heritage rediscovered ; 42)
Includes bibliographical references.
ISBN 9789351481454 (HB)
ISBN 9789351481461 (PB)

1. Vilappilsala Janakeeya Samithy (Vilappilsala, India). 2. Trivandrum (India) 3. Refuse and refuse disposal--India--Trivandrum. 4. Protest movements--India--Vilappilsala. 5. Sustainable urban development--India--Trivandrum. 6. Ecotheology--India--Kerala. I. Title. II. Series: Christian heritage rediscovered ; 42.

TD789.I42T75 2016 DDC 363.728095483 23

Printed in India.

Dedicated to...
my late grandmother Lalitha who taught me
the values of simple life
and also to
the countless victims of garbage crisis...

Contents

Acknowledgements

First of all, I thank God, the true inspiration of my life and wisdom for enabling me to pursue my M.Th Studies in Social Analysis.

This book in its original form is the thesis submitted to the Senate of Serampore College towards my Master of Theology degree. I am thankful to the Senate for granting me permission to publish the same. I am solely responsible for the changed title, contents and opinions expressed in it.

I express my sincere gratitude to my research guide Rev. Dr. Solomon Victus who offered his valuable suggestions, critical comments and immeasurable encouragement that helped me to broaden my perspectives.

I am very much thankful to the Tamil Nadu Theological Seminary, Madurai especially Principal Rev. Dr. M. Gnanavaram, Rev. Dr. Margaret Kalaiselvi, the Dean of Post Graduate Studies, Rev. Dr. J. David Rajendran, the HOD, the Department of Social Analysis and Rev. Dr. John Jeyaharan for their valuable academic and practical performances, which influenced me.

I extend my sincere thanks to library staff of DSA, especially Jayaseelakka, Prabhu, Mani and Elizabeth, TTS General Library, University Library and Public Library, Thiruvananthapuram for the help in accessing sufficient research materials.

I am deeply indebted to the CSI South Kerala Diocese for providing me enough study leave to complete my studies. I am particularly thankful to CSI Kulumala and its members for remembering me in their prayers and their encouragement.

I am specially obliged to my grandfather, N. Johannan, my mother, Suseelabai and brother R. Shiju and cousin, Rev. Shine P. K, who have upheld me in their prayers, and encouraged me to continue studies. I am thankful to my father-in-law, Rev. B.E. Selvamoni Raj and Sanumathy Raj, the mother-in-law for taking care of my family in my absence and for their moral support.

I am grateful to Reeja, Rev. William Allbery, Sonu George, Rev. Philip George, Rev. Prasanth S. P., Rev. Saju Kumar. U, Rev. David Gladson, Reuban, Rev. Lingala Samuel, Rev. Biju Cherian, Leitaim for their sound insights, Sunil Singh, Manjuly, Jujan, Ramkoti, Daniel Gnaprakasam, Daniel Edwin, Rev. T. C. Thomas Shine and Lal Raj for their care and support.

I express my sincere thanks to Rev. Dr. C. I. David Joy, the New Testament scholar from UTC, Bangaluru for his encouragement in publishing my thesis.

I thankfully remember Rev. Anilal M. Jose for the idea of cover design.

Beyond words to express my profound gratitude and heartfelt thanks to my life partner and friend Dr. Deepa Shibu, who has given sacrificial service during my studies and children Viwa and Vian who had showed me their understanding.

No words are sufficient to express my gratitude to Christian World Imprints, who transformed my research into a book form.

Preface

The history of human civilization is also the history of waste generation and disposal whether success or failure. It starts from the very moment when life is created and passed through diverse societies ranging from the primitive to the modern industrial era and is still continuing. It becomes a problem when there is even a small hindrance in the management of waste. This happened in Thiruvananthapuram also.

The Thiruvananthapuram Corporation wanted to get rid of the issue of waste accumulation by selecting a rural place, Vilappilsala, for the construction of a waste treatment plant. Topographically the place is unfit for the plant because of its proximity to a low lying water source which became unfit even for cattle washing. In this context the Vilappilsala Janakeeya Samithy (VJS), a people's movement, mobilized the people and intensified the struggle which ultimately led to the closure of the plant. This book **Zero Waste Economy: Theological Insights for Urban Sustainable Waste Management** is an attempt to study the conflict between VJS and the Corporation on the question of waste disposal. The author made use of the quantitative method under which questionnaires were distributed and interviews done with the villagers and the Corporation authorities to find out the real facts, and the data collected was codified and analysed under Houtart's Method of Social Analysis.

The research work is divided into five chapters: the first chapter deals with the evolution of the concept of waste, the Indian context of waste disposal and its caste origin, the history of the waste situation in Kerala, how waste became a problem in Thiruvananthapuram, why the Corporation preferred Vilappilsala as the dumping site and established a solid waste treatment plant, the evolution of the people's movement, various protests initiatives, and the formation of the VJS.

The second chapter focuses on the background study of Vilappil village, why the Corporation failed to run the plant, the nature of the struggles led by the VJS, the response of the Panchayat, Corporation and the State Government to the struggle, etc. They used various local methods for leading the resistance. However, the Corporation retaliated by putting false cases and arresting the leaders of the struggle.

The third chapter is a study on 'the impact of the plant on the life of the villagers' in various spheres and the analysis of the data. The leachate from the plant polluted the water, caused the air to stink and attracted rodents, stray dogs, birds and big swarms of flies; it caused health problems, failures of marriage proposals, the growth of land mafia taking advantage of the local people's tendency to sell their land, etc., and persistently threatened their lives. Despite such impacts, the people were cautious against the politics between different governing bodies over their issue, the tendency to hijack the struggle and so on.

The fourth chapter, speaks about how the solid waste problem was worsened, especially by the use of plastic and how to address the issue through 'four R's and one L'; a discussion is made on the importance of 'reduce, reuse, recycle, reject and landfill' under the integrated waste management and suggests the importance of alternatives such as the use of decomposable plastic, the use of cloth bags, preferring unpackaged and durable products, source level disposal of waste etc.

The final chapter is a 'theological reflection on waste management.' It deals with the concept of *good* and *holiness*, and the *burial* system of human excreta and dead bodies, the issue of *burning* of wood, burning of carcasses, smoke, hell as burning fire, *dumping/landfilling* of the artefacts in the Kidron valley, *alternative use of waste* as the use of waste fuel pellets, *the waste concept of Judas* and *Jesus as resisting a throw away consumerist culture,* and finally the development of a new theology of waste management as the 'zero waste theology.'

The struggle in Vilappilsala raises serious questions about the nature of consumerism and the resultant generation of waste. Waste accumulation is the result of consumerist culture and its dumping in rural areas is the consequence of the NIMBY (not in my backyard) syndrome of the urban dwellers. The Vilappilsala struggle was for their survival, quite apart from an ecological issue. Even the VJS members were not ready to sacrifice their middle class benefits for waste reduction. The remarkable thing in their struggle was their unity in organizing themselves which could encourage other movements leading similar struggles. It is true that complete rejection of consumerism is a difficult task, so a minimalistic way of living is essential. An the attitudinal change is required to consider 'my waste, my property and my responsibility'; the government's political will is required to limit the use of plastic products and wrappings; and people's movements, NGOs and religious organizations to mobilize people against consumerism are all required to create a zero-waste economy.

List of Abbreviations

AAI	:	Airport Authority of India
AC	:	Advocate Commission
AD	:	Anna Dominie
ADB	:	Asian Development Bank
ADM	:	Additional District Magistrate
Adv.	:	Advocate
AMCHSS	:	Achutha Menon Centre for Health Science Studies
AP	:	Andhra Pradesh
BCE	:	Before Christian Era
BOO	:	Build Own Operate
CBO	:	Community Based Organization
CE	:	Christian Era
CED	:	Centre for Environment and Development
CHC	:	Community Health Centre
CM	:	Chief Minister
CrPC	:	Code of Criminal Procedure
CSI	:	Church of South India
DMO	:	District Medical Officer
ECC	:	Ecumenical Christian Centre
EM	:	Essential Microbeum
FACT	:	Fertilizers and Chemicals Limited

FRAN	:	Federation of Residents Association Neyyatinkara
GO	:	Government Order
IWM	:	Integrated Waste Management
KHC	:	Kerala High Court
KS	:	Karma Samithy
KSPCB	:	Kerala State Pollution Control Board
LDF	:	Left Democratic Front
Ltd.	:	Limited
MD	:	Managing Director
MLA	:	Member of Legislative Assembly
MO	:	Medical Officer
MoUD	:	Ministry of Urban Development
MP	:	Member of Parliament
NCC	:	Nadar Co- Ordination Committee
NGO	:	Non Government Organization
PCB	:	Pollution Control Board
PS	:	Paura Samithy
Pvt.	:	Private
RC	:	Roman Catholic
RTI	:	Right to Information
SC	:	Supreme Court
SEWA	:	Self Employed Women's Association
SKD	:	South Kerala Diocese
SNDP	:	Sri Narayana Dharma Paripalana
SSS	:	Samyuktha Samara Samithy
SUCI	:	Social Unity Centre of India
SWM	:	Solid Waste Management
TV	:	Television
USA	:	United States of America
VAC	:	Vilappilsala Action Council
VJS	:	Vilappilsala Janakeeya Samithy

List of Glossary

Dharna	:	A demonstration usually done by people as a symbol of protest.
Hartaal	:	Closing shops and institutions as a symbol of protest.
Malayalees	:	People who were born in Kerala and speak Malayalam language.
Pongala	:	Sweet pudding usually cooked by women in connection with temple festivals as a symbol of appeasing the presiding deity.
Samara Pandal	:	A temporary shed used to shelter agitators.
Saree	:	Long upper garment worn by women.
Satyagraha	:	A Sanskrit word meaning 'adhering to truth'. It is a non-violent form of people's protest.
Shawl	:	Piece of cloth used by women to cover their head, shoulder and breast.

Introduction

Waste, solid, liquid or gaseous in form, is the most unwelcome residue that everybody wants to get rid of. The well-being of a person, community or a nation depends on how we dispose of waste, the failure of which can lead to waste accumulation. Solid waste disposal is a major problem in the urbanized world. Kerala, the southernmost State of India, is also becoming a victim of dumping of solid waste by its own people. The impasse in solid waste disposal and treatment is actually felt in various Corporations of Kochi, Kozhikode and the Municipalities of Kannoor and Thalessery.[1] Solid waste disposal in Thiruvananthapuram District has become a major challenge to the city Corporation, which needs a careful study for which this thesis makes an attempt.

1. Background of the Research

The Thiruvanathapuram Corporation has established a solid waste treatment plant in Vilappilsala, a rural area, 14 km away from the village to counter the city's aggravate waste crisis. The health issues created by the plant made the people to organize and to resist the plant as well as the Corporation under the people's movement, Vilappilsala Janakeeya Samithy (VJS). This conflict is studied within the frame work of the viable ecologically sustainable system of urban

1 Mohamed Nazeer, "A Crisis in Highly Urbanized Kerala," *The Hindu* (Madurai), 12 August 2012, 11.

waste disposal. Biblical theological insights for safe and sustainable waste disposal will be attempted.

2. Definition

Solid waste has been defined as a "heterogeneous mass of useless material, which may originate from homes or commercial or industrial activities."[2] The management of solid waste has meant the management of the flow stream of waste from generation to disposal through the process of collection, transportation, processing and final disposal.[3]

3. An Elaboration

The solid waste treatment plant in Vilappilsala was started on July 24, 2000[4], with private participation for processing biodegradable waste into manure, but it failed over the dispute of price and leachate generation. Its management went through different companies, Government agencies and finally the Corporation, but they all failed to contain air, land and water pollutions. As the plant is situated on a hillock, the leachate from the garbage polluted the neighbouring water sources such as wells and especially streams which open into the nearby Karamana river on which the majority of the urban and rural population depends on for drinking water. Moreover, swarming of flies, epidemics, chronic diseases and stench from the plant make the life of the people difficult.

On realizing that not only they but the future generation would also be affected by the plant, the villagers, under the VJS, started organizing against the polluting plant demanding its closure. The impasse in waste treatment has turned the people's movement and the Panchayat against the City Corporation and the State Government. The author tried to focus on the conflict between the solid waste disposal plant in Thiruvananthapuram city and the people's struggles

2 K.N Nair and Sridhar R, eds., *Cleaning Up Kerala. Studies in Self- help in Dealing with Solid Waste* (Delhi: Daanish Books, 2005), 1.

3 Ibid.

4 *Malayala Manorama* (Thiruvananthapuram), 21 September 2011, 3.

to close it, and the search for sustainable alternatives to the problem of solid waste disposal.

The theology that emerges from the study of garbology states that whatever God created is 'good' and 'holy.' Evil is powerful and there is also a fear of destruction and contamination. The 'good' is considered sacred and useful; and the useless is waste and therefore must be thrown out. The management of waste is to keep our environment 'good' and 'holy.' This can be done through various means such as reducing usage, recycling or reusing and making the waste organic/degradable and thus returning it to nature so that nature can easily assimilate it.[5] And it is also essential to consider others when seeking solutions for the disposal of garbage.

4. Significance of the Research

Waste, both decomposing and non-decomposing, is a pollutant. It is harmful to the environment but also to the inhabitants. So the study of waste accumulation as one of the causes of pollution, the methods of management of solid waste, the problem its mismanagement creates and its alternatives, need to be done thoroughly. Reduced value of housing plots and migration to other areas are two of the few challenges that the people have experienced. It has affected their normal life creating health hazards. As a theological student, the author is obliged to recall that, we, being created in God's own image and likeness, are stewards of creation. The research is important for motivating people facing various issues to stand firm in protest against any projects affecting their peaceful life. Though this project affects the people of one village named Vilappil, it is a sensitive issue in Kerala because the actions of the villagers can motivate people all around the State to be united to protect their normal life.

5. Method of Research

This research is based on the quantitative method. Questionnaires were prepared to have a general survey on what dimensions the waste

5 John. E (Jack) Swanson, "Garbage Theology: Findings of a Garbologist/Theologian/Environmentalist," http://www.webofcreations.org (07 August 2012).

disposal crisis impacted, to evaluate people's attitude to the issue, and to enable an in-depth study on the impact of the plant, on the life of the villagers and the workers of the plant, and how it affected their health, livelihood, socio-political conditions etc. Interviews with workers of the plant, villagers, protestors as well as the Corporation authorities were also done to get transparency of information. These were used as primary sources. The data collected were codified and analyzed.

Waste disposal is not merely seen as a technical, scientific issue. It is linked with the material base which not only involves the use of resources and market mechanisms but also ensures the rejuvenation of nature and its sustainability. It deals with political structures and ideological and religious meanings implied in the choice of waste disposal along with the health and social well-being of city dwellers as well as those who are at the receiving end.

6. Methodology

These interlinkages between the material base, collective life and symbolic representation are analysed using the framework of Francois Houtart's Methodology of Social Analysis. The author focuses only on the material base such as the socio-economic factors, the collective life in relation to the role of the State, civil society and the people's movement, and symbolic representation, i.e., religion and ideology.

7. Previous Research

Abraham P. George of Achutha Menon Centre for Health Science Studies (AMCHSS) wrote a P.G thesis on *Solid Waste Management in Thiruvananthapuram City: A Case Study* in 2000 under the Shree Chithra Institute of Medical Science and Technology based on medical aspects. But this research concentrated on the conflict between the Vilappilsala Janakeeya Samithy and the question of solid waste disposal in Thiruvananthapuram and the search for ecologically sustainable alternatives.

8. Scope and Limitation

Solid waste management has become a major concern of the globe, and nowadays the states as well as people are thinking about how to overcome the problem. It is a wider issue, and many places in Kerala also have the same problem. So, the author wanted to limit the study to Thiruvananthapuram city within the stipulated time.

9. Chapterization

The first chapter, deals with the evolution of waste situation in India, complexity of garbage problem in Kerala, especially Thiruvananthapuram and the problems relating to the disposal of solid waste in Vilappilsala.

The second chapter, describes why the solid waste treatment plant failed, how did the VJS lead the struggle and what kind of response did they get from the Corporation, State Government, etc.

The third chapter analyses the problems that the people in Vilappilsala had to face using the Houtart Methodology of Social Analysis.

The fourth chapter, focuses on what multidimensional approach can be utilized as a solution to the accumulating waste crisis.

And the fifth chapter develops a theology of waste management and finally the conclusion.

Chapter 1

History of Waste Disposal in Trivandrum and Conflict with Vilappilsala Janakeeya Samithy

1. Introduction

Waste is one of the most disreputable hindrances which everyone has to deal with. Waste generation starts from human body itself to the biggest industries. The welfare of a community as well as environment depends on how we dispose of waste. It becomes a matter of conflict with improper management. Every country, state or city are still experiencing crisis in the management of waste. Kerala is not an exception. The capital city Thiruvanathapuram is also experiencing the same problem which the Corporation has been struggling to tackle for more than a decade. They have started a solid waste treatment plant in Vilappilsala, in the outskirts of the city, but its operation creates so many problems to the villagers. This chapter is an attempt to search the background of solid waste disposal in Thiruvanathapuram and the evolution of people's resistance.

1.1 Waste

Waste is an unavoidable part of human activities. In primitive societies, the waste produced was human and animal excreta, and bones and carcasses thrown out by hunters, which was later absorbed by the earth.[6] The abandonment of nomadic life at around 10,000 BCE and the starting of community life saw the beginning of the accumulation of waste. However they tried to manage this problem through different means. The rubbish chutes in Mohenjo-Daro, toilets and drains in Harappa and Punjab, trunk sewers connecting homes in the island of Crete in 2100 BCE , the sanitary laws of Moses in 1600 BCE , the sewers in old Jerusalem in 200 BCE, etc. were the instances of primitive waste disposal systems.[7] Waste accumulated in the streets and around the towns in Rome in 14 CE.[8] The situation became more complex with the industrial revolution which had turned waste as a major product of human consumption.[9] The developed countries tried to sort out the issue of waste accumulation by either dumping into the sea or sending barges full of waste into third world countries. The capitalists prospered in the industry by producing one time use flimsy articles, funding the *civilizing missions*[10] to market their products among the natives.[11] These cheap articles turned out to be waste. They penetrated the democratic countries and propagated the ideology of development

6 Salahuddin Mohd, *Waste Management in an Urban Area* (Delhi: B.R. Publishing Corporation, 2011), v.

7 P. Arne Vesilund, William Worrel and Reinhart, *Solid Waste Engineering* (Bangalore: Bill Stenquist, 2002), 1.

8 V. K. Prabhakar, ed., *Solid Waste Management* (New Delhi: Anmol Publications Pvt. Ltd., 2001), 5.

9 Ibid.

10 The capitalist made use of missionaries to promote the sale of their products. They describe the newly found people as uncivilized/ barbarians who were depending on the traditional wares for their sustenance. The missionaries used the ideology of civilizing the people through which capitalists found market for their products.

11 Bharathan Kumarappa, *Capitalism, Socialism or Villagism?* (Varanasi: Sarva Seva Sangh Prakashan, 1965), 17-21.

by luring consumers through advertisements, fashions, high standard of living, etc.[12] All these promoted rapid urbanization making India also as a victim to a consumerist culture which created waste accumulation problems. The municipalities which were supposed to do waste management could not satisfactorily do it as they ran out of funds. This has increased waste the accumulation problem in Indian cities.

1.1.1 *Definition of Waste*

All beings including humans and well as creatures make decisions about what to use and what to throw away. This thrown away substance is called waste. Waste is defined as, "consequence of everyday life."[13] The German Waste Act defines waste as, "any portable objects that have been abandoned by its owner(s), or requiring orderly disposal to protect the public welfare."[14] According to New Zealand Waste Strategy, waste is, "any material, solid, liquid or gas that is unwanted and /or unvalued and discarded or discharged by its owner."[15] Based on its form waste can be classified into different states.

1.1.2 *Types of Waste*

Waste is generated either mainly by human activities or animal excreta which are either solid or liquid in nature leading to land or water pollution. The solid waste generally arises from heterogeneous bulk of rejected or thrown away substances and also from heterogeneous accumulation of waste produced by agricultural or industrial activities.[16] Waste produced in this manner can be categorized as municipal waste/solid waste, hospital waste, industrial waste and

12 Kumarappa, op.cit., 25-27.

13 Vesilund, op.cit.

14 T. V. Ramachandran, "Management of Municipal Solid Waste: Strategies" (Manuscript of a lecture delivered at Bangalore ECC Seminar on solid waste management, 25 September 2012).

15 Ibid.

16 Suresh K. Dhameja, *Environment Engineering and Management* (New Delhi: S. K. Kataria and Sons, 2002), 172.

so on.[17] All these are based on the sources from where they are produced.

1.1.3 *Solid Waste*

Municipal waste, otherwise called solid waste, can be defined as a heterogeneous mass of useless material which may originate from homes or commercial activities.[18] "It includes mostly household/ domestic waste with sometimes the addition of commercial waste collected by a municipality within a given area."[19] The Resource Conservation and Recovery Act of USA defines solid waste as "any garbage, refuse, sludge from waste treatment plant, water supply treatment plant, or air pollution control facility and other discarded material, including solid, liquid, semi-solid, or contained gaseous material resulting from industrial, commercial, mining and agricultural operation, and from community activities."[20] It can be classified as the following types[21] such as the garbage or food waste, rubbish, agricultural waste, industrial waste, hazardous waste, miscellaneous waste like street sweepings and litter, demolition waste, aquatic waste, medical waste, etc.

1.1.4 *Solid Waste Management (SWM)*

Solid waste management is the management of the flow stream of waste from generation to disposal through the process of collection, transportation and finally disposal.[22] It is the minimization or reduction of solid waste and adversely impacts on health, environment, and the aesthetic quality of landscape. All nations, whether developing or developed in nature, have been obliged to

---

17 K. N. Nair and Sridhar R, eds., *Cleaning Up Kerala. Studies in Self-help in Dealing with Solid Waste* (Delhi: Daanish Books, 2005), 6-8.

18 Ibid.

19 P. N. Prasad and T. R. Amarnath, *Waste Pollution and Its Control* (New Delhi: Crescent Publishing Corporation, 2010), 3.

20 Ramachandran, op. cit.

21 Dhameja, op. cit., 172-173.

22 Nair, op. cit., 1.

manage the solid waste produced within them. The Indian situation is not an exception and it needs a detailed analysis.

1.2 The Indian Context of Waste Situation

From the Vedic period itself, nothing was considered waste in India. Household waste was either fed to cattle or become part of manure or pushed to the outskirts of cities or composted in dumping pits which later became manure for agricultural farms. Later the waste situation emerged with the caste system in Hinduism in the post-Vedic period. The caste Hindus sidelined a fifth group of people who were considered outside the *four varna system.*[23] They were called the untouchables or the Dalits, supposed to do filthy jobs such as digging graves, disposing dead animals, cleaning human waste with bare hands and so on.[24] The practice got a little modification as Britishers tried to introduce hygienic practices. *Night soil*[25] from dry latrines was collected by scavengers and was buried in trenches.[26] This situation had undergone tremendous changes in the post-Independence India with the advent of industrialization and the resultant consumerist practices. This had far reaching effects across India and particularly in Kerala.

1.3 History of Waste Situation in Kerala

Kerala claims to be very high in literacy, personal hygiene and health, but low in environmental consciousness and public sanitation. It had a tradition of honouring the environment. However, scavenging in

---

23 They were the Brahmins, the Kshathriyas, the Vaisyars and the Sudras. The Brahmins were the priestly class, the Kshathriyas the ruling class, the Vaisyars the commoners or the free farmers and the Shudras were the labourers and the service providers.

24 Robert Cooke, "The Caste System of India," *Trinicenter Special*, http://www.race and history.com/historicalviews/casteindia.htm (18 November 2013).

25 This is a euphemistic term for human excreta.

26 Almitra H. Patel, Member, the Supreme Court Committe for Solid Waste Management in Class 1 Cities, "Urban Solid Waste Management: Progress and Prospects for Social, Technical and Policy Improvement," http://www.almitrapatel.com (19 August 2013).

towns and open defecation in village areas were generally accepted.[27] Thiruvananthapuram became the first city in India to impose a ban on manual scavenging in 1958.[28] The waste crisis situation in Kerala aroused after 1970s with the advent of the Gulf boom. *Malayalees*[29] went to the Middle East and brought back a lot of consumer goods, built new houses, commercial establishments, etc., which boosted the consumerist pattern in the State.

1.3.1 *Consumerism and Waste in Kerala*

Consumerism is the mode of consumption on a large scale of imported goods.[30] The craze for consumerism created a large quantum of urban inorganic waste which was toxic and infectious in nature in Kerala.[31] Before that the only organic waste which needed to be disposed was the night soil, collected in the morning and disposed of

27 Thrivikramji. K.P., "Kerala's Baby Steps Toward Sanitation: The Vilappilsala Plant," http://www.trivikramji.com (12 February 2012).

28 *Development of Trivandrum Municipality and Corporation* (Thiruvananthapuram: Thiruvananthapuram Nagarasabha, 1998), 9.

29 The term means the people of Kerala speaking Malayalam language.

30 John Desroches, *The India We Want to Build*, vol. 2 (Bangalore: Centre for Social Action, 1995), 83.

31 There are different reasons for the emergence of consumerism in Kerala. (i) The British presence made people to be the victims of foreign goods, commercialization of agriculture and the exploitation of forest resources, (ii) the migration to West Asia, (iii) the development of construction sectre, (iv) the generation of IT related employment, all of which have brought disposable income and love for consumer goods, (v) the influence of Enlightenment and Romanticism bringing changes in the thinking pattern, (vi) the changes in the dressing pattern, (vii) the disappearance of urban- rural divide, (viii) social reforms bringing disintegration of caste hierarchy, creating a middle class society, (ix) the spread of education and imitation of the western style, (x) the shopping mall culture, (xi) the governmental policies, (xii) the influence of media, (xiii) the multiplication of credit facilities, (xiv) the impact of tourism, (xiii) the creation of public pseudo spaces like theatres, etc. M. P. Abdulla, "Trends, Causes and Consequences of Consumerism in Kerala" (2008), Department of Economics, University of Calicut. http://www.shodhganga.inflibnet.ac.in/handle/10603/594 (30 September 2013).

in the central dumping yard.[32] Market and other Corporation waste was usually purchased by farmers for cultivation as it contained only bio-degradable waste, but the situation changed with the arrival of non-biodegradable waste such as plastic and other toxic waste.[33] All these conditions have made waste management a difficult problem. Till now the state has not attained self sufficiency in resolving the crisis created by the waste expelled by the huge population.

1.4 Population

Kerala has five Corporations, 60 municipalities and 978 gram panchayats.[34] The provisional population figures of 2011 estimate 17,455,506 and 15,932,171 people in the rural and urban areas respectively.[35] The population of Thiruvananthapuram Corporation is 7,52,490 of which 3,64,657 are males and 3,87,833 are females.[36] The Government's statistics show the State is generating 8300 tonnes of garbage per day.[37] Vilappil Panchayat has a population of 34,079 persons of them 16,740 are males and 17,339 are females and it consists of 8147 households.[38] The present problem is that, the existing technology is insufficient to manage all the waste produced per day in Kerala which augmented the solid waste.

1.5 Solid Waste Management Crisis in Kerala

Various places in Kerala are under the menace of solid waste accumulation. Major Corporations such as Thiruvananthapuram,

---

32 Nair, op. cit., 6-8.

33 Interview with Shiva Kailas, Convenor, Samyuktha Samara Samithy, 14 April 2013.

34 http://www.keralagov.in (17 July 2013)..

35 In the rural population 8,403,706 are males and 9,051,800 are females and the urban population consists of 7,617,584 males and 8,314,587 females. Ibid.

36 http://www.censusindia.gov.in (17 July 2013).

37 "Keralamenna Malinyakoomparam," *Malayala Manorama* (Thiruvananthapuram), 2 July 2013, 10.

38 http://www.censusindia.gov.in, op. cit.

Kollam, Cochin, Trissur, Kozhikode and other municipalities are in conflict with rural people for their resistance over the disposal of city waste into their backyards. Waste disposal in north Kerala especially, Laloor, Brahmapuram and Njeliyambra has been affected for so long following people's protest.[39] In the central Kerala, waste disposal in Vadavathoor in Kottayam still remains unresolved even after 70 years of dumping. In southern part, Kureepuzha in Kollam and Vilappilsala in Thiruvananthapuram are also facing a solid waste management crisis.[40]

The rapid change in consumption patterns and the growth of the service sector have also been responsible for the waste management crisis in Kerala. An analysis of the figures can reveal how much waste Kerala is producing and how we have to tackle this situation.

1.6 Statistics of Solid Waste Generation in Kerala

Recent statistics reveal that Kerala is expelling 8,300 tonnes of waste per day in which 85% of municipal solid waste is organic.[41] At the individual level, in urban areas an average of 200-400 gm and in rural area 8-10 gm of waste is being generated per day per head.[42] It is a simple thing to handle such a small quantity of waste at the source itself, but its negligence and failure lead to unimaginable solid waste accumulation. However, there are good instances of solid waste management in some part of the State.

---

39 In Laloor people have been agitating more than two years. Vadavukode, Puthencruz and Kunnathunadu panchayats are still protesting over Brahmapuram garbage treatment plant. Protests are on the rise in Njeliyambra for the Kozhikode Corporation where the people are demanding to upgrade the garbage treatment plant so as to prevent leachate flow and to get a new landfill site. Nazeer, op.cit.

40 "Pollution Near Kureepuzha Alarming: Study," *The Hindu* (13 August 2011), http://www.thehindu.com/todays-paper/tp-national/tp-kerala/pollution-near-kureepuzha-alarming-study/article2352864. ece (5 March 2014).

41 "Keralamenna Malinyakoomparam," op. cit.

42 M. Suchithra and P. N. Venugopal, "Malinyam Valarunnu, Athirukal Kadannum," *Mathrubhumi Azhchapathippu* 50/84 (2 February 2007): 24.

1.7 Good Instances of SWM in Kerala

Despite negligence in SWM, there are instances of effective management of solid waste in Kerala. Shoranur, Kodungalloor and Attingal municipalities are scientifically doing garbage treatment. The Shoranur municipality has planted 100 biogas plants.[43] The garbage treatment plant in Attingal is producing 200 kgs of vermiform compost per tonne in an area of 3.06 acres.[44] Besides, a biogas plant and plastic shredding unit are processing 16 tonnes of garbage a day.[45] The success of these plants depends on the selection of the place that is a low lying area, strictly adhering to scientific expert opinion and people's participation in the collection and depositing waste at the municipality collection centres and conscientization, the failure of which can aggravate the waste situation.

1.8 The Peculiarity of Kerala in Relation to SWM

Kerala is fortunate to have rain for about half a year. If rain water happens to mix with liquid and solid food items, they decompose. Kerala's topography, population density, unscientific methods of construction habits, consumption patterns and little care for our habitat are the culprits for solid waste accumulation, which impacted in Thiruvananthapuram also.

1.9 Consumerist Pattern and Waste Context in Thiruvananthapuram

Thiruvananthapuram, the capital of Kerala, has been considered as one of the cleanest and the most educated people living cities in Kerala. It became the capital of Travancore in 1750.[46] Even after the formation of Kerala State on 1 November 1956,

---

43 Sarah Joseph, "Nagarathinte Kuppathottikal," *Madhyamam Azhchapathippu* 734/15 (12 March 2012): 25.

44 Vijayan Palazhi, "Attingaline Kandu Padikku," *Kerala Kaumudi* (Thiruvananthapuram), 10 January 2012, 11.

45 M. Pradeep, "Malinya Samskarana Mikavu," *Malayala Manorama* (Thiruvananthapuram), 5 June 2013, 10.

46 http://www.corporationoftrivandrum.in (17 July 2013).

Thiruvananthapuram remained the headquarters of the State. This needed more institutions and created more waste. By the 1970s there was a shift in the consumerist pattern in Thiruvananthapuram, like other places of Kerala. The use of plastic and packaged products and the attempts to dispose of the accumulating dry domestic waste by burning and dumping in uninhabited places, water sources as the Karamana river and drainages increased waste crisis in the city. The Corporation used to collect garbage from various markets within the city and dumping in Vallakadavu, near Thiruvananthapuram airport. It came to a standstill by a Government Order in 1985 following a complaint by the Airport Authority of India (AAI) on the ground that birds from this place posed a threat to low flying aircrafts.[47] The dumping of waste in slum areas also met with resistance. In this context it became the responsibility of the Corporation to tackle the rising solid waste crisis.

1.10 The Thiruvananthapuram Corporation

As a solution to the accumulating solid waste problem the Corporation started a garbage treatment plant in Vilappilsala in 2000. At its initial stage, the transportation of waste to the plant was done in uncovered vehicles during nights.[48] Pesticides worse than endosulfan were sprayed on the garbage heap.[49] They also claimed that the FACT would purchase manure produced from the factory.[50] The Corporation tried to drive away various apprehensions of the villagers through discussions and public meetings.[51] They brought

47 Thrivikramji, op. cit.

48 V. Jayaprakash, "Mathrikaparamaya Pravarthanam," *Malayala Manorama* (Thiruvananthapuram), 25 July 2010, 9.

49 "Vilappilsalayile Malinya Prasnathil Ettumuttal Sakthamakunnu," *Mathrubhumi* (Thiruvananthapuram), 9 February 2011, 12.

50 G. R. Anil, "Kendra Sarkar Kuttakkar," *Malayala Manorama* (Thiruvananthapuram), 25 July 2010, 9.

51 They organized a public meeting and discussion at the Vilappilsala Upper Primary School on 28 November 1999. The Mayor, the District Collector, the Corporation Secretary, people's representatives and more than 2000 people participated in the discussion. J. C. Johnson, "Diary Writings," Vilappilsala.

a team to visit the Vijayawada solid waste treatment plant to rule out people's concerns, but the convincing of which depended on corruption in terms of money and liquor.[52] Apart from that, the Corporation gave a set of unfulfilled promises to the people to get their support.

1.10.1 *Major Promises of the Corporation*

In an undated brochure released by the Corporation prior to the inauguration of the plant, the Corporation enlisted eleven promises.[53] They were:

- i. The focus on generation of electricity from waste.
- ii. The construction of the plant in the middle of 13 acres.
- iii. No dumping of waste from hospital and slaughter houses.
- iv. Planting of trees in and around the factory to prevent air pollution.
- v. The construction of a protective wall to prevent the pollution of drinking water in the nearby water sources.
- vi. The dumping pits of everyday waste would be daily covered with soil with the help of an excavator.
- vii. Only covered vehicles would be used for the transportation of waste.
- viii. The Corporation owned property would be protected with compound and iron walls.
- ix. The plant will function without making any disturbance to the neighbouring people as it uses modern technology.

---

52 On 17 October 1996 a five member team, consisting of the then Thiruvananthapuram M. P., K. V. Surendranath, M.L.A. Venganoor Bhaskaran, Mayor V. Sivankutty, District Collector Aruna Sudararaj and Corporation Secretary M. Najeeb visited the plant in Vijayawada. Since they were convinced of the functioning of plant, the Corporation authorities brought the Vilappil panchayat members as well as the representatives of the Action Council to the Vijayawada plant as per their promise. They also visited the plant and were fully convinced of the efficiency of the plant, but regarding the Vilappilsala plant, it proved to be the most inefficient plant.

53 "Vaidyudi Utpadanam Chavaril Ninum," Pamphlet, Corporation, (Thiruvananthapuram) 2000.

x. Instead of a dumping yard, it would be a solid waste treatment plant, which the Mayor made clear.[54]

xi. It would start, after getting a positive nod from the Ministry of Environment, in the model of Vijayawada plant.[55]

Of all these promises only ii, v and viii were met. On the other hand important things were neglected and the Corporation did not keep its promises. Instead they wanted to stick on their motto.

1.10.2 *The Motto of the Corporation*

The motto of the Corporation was fundamentally modern development and urbanization for which the villagers also had a role to play. The Corporation held that 'today's city was yesterday's village, and yesterday's village would be tomorrow's city.[56] It was running after technology and development at the cost of the villagers. It also used the ownership of land to justify all its aims. There were different social and economic factors which contributed to the pursuance of the Corporation's vested interests of which the Clean City Green City Project and the Asian Development Bank play major roles.

1.11 'Clean City, Green City' Project and Asian Development Bank Loan

In 1996, the Government wanted to implement the 'Clean City, Green City project' through different Corporations. As part of the project the Corporation found a place, Vilappilsala for establishing a garbage treatment plant. It got an impetus when the State Government took the Asian Development Bank (ADB) loan of 1084 crore rupees in 2006 when the Left Democratic Front (LDF) was in power. The main objective was utilizing the fund for water supply,

---

54 "Vilappilsalayil Dumping Yard Thudangilla," *Malayala Ma*norama (Thiruvananthapuram), 5 October 1996, 3.

55 "Vilappilslayil Dumping Yard Illa, Pakaram Valam Factory," *Mathrubhumi* (Thiruvananthapuram), 5 October 1996, 7.

56 "Vaidyudi Utpadanam Chavaril Ninum," op. cit.

transport, sewage expulsion and solid waste management.[57] Most of the amount was lapsed because of non-spending and lack of proper plans. Even though Vilappilsala plant also was benefitted from this loan, the Corporation could not achieve its goals which ultimately led to the problems in Vilappilsala.

1.12 Solid Waste Treatment Plant in Vilappilsala

The solid waste treatment plant in Vilappilsala was an initiative of the Thiruvananthapuram Corporation for a solution to the city's rising garbage problem generated by a population of 5,24,000.[58] It was inaugurated by the then Chief Minister (CM) E. K. Nayanar on 24 July 2000.[59] It was modelled on the Vijayawada solid waste treatment plant. Its history extended to a period of nearly two decades.

1.12.1 *History of the Vilappilsala Plant*

The history of Vilappilsala solid waste treatment plant is also the history of deception. In 1993 the Corporation bought an area of 18.6 hectares of land in Chowalloor ward of Vilappil village under the leadership of the then Mayor V. Sivankuttuy using the pretext of starting a herbal garden. The protests of the people were silenced by the Corporation using police arrests on false charges.[60] In this context the villagers were assured that the plant would be pollution free and run under the supervision of scientific experts.[61] However none of the assurances were kept.

57 C. R. Neelakandan, "Gramathil Kondupoyi Illathakkunna 'Prasnam'," *Mathrubhumi Azhchapathippu* 48/89 (February 11-17, 2012): 28.

58 M. Shankar, "Keralam Oru Pannikoodu," *Samakalika Malayalam Varika* (25 October 2002): 16.

59 N. Vasudevan Nair, "Vilappilsalaykku 10 Vayassu," *Malayala Manorama* (Thiruvananthapuram), 25 July 2012, 9.

60 Interview with Johnson, A Resident, Vilappilsala, 20 April 2013.

61 M. Suchithra, "Stench in My Backyard," *Down to Earth* 21/8 (September 1-15, 2012): 28-34.

1.12.2 *Parameters of the Solid Waste Treatment Plant*

The plant consisted of a main roofed building of 1,10,000 sq.ft. As with the Vijayawada plant, the operational charge of the Vilappilsala plant was given to the Excel Industries under Poabson. Unlike the Vijayawada plant, the roofing made it different to prevent leachate flow. From different times the responsibility of operating the plant was given to Poabson Envirotech, the Centre for Environment Development and finally the Corporation itself directly started to handle the plant making the running of the plant problematic.

1.12.3 *Poabson Envirotech (Pvt.) Ltd.*

Poabson Envirotech was the first to run the plant, under which the Excel Industries had to manage the processes of waste treatment. It is less bothered about *environmental destruction.*[62] The Company was selected on the basis of tender under 'build, own and operate (B.O.O).'[63] Poabson was supposed to use the city waste for making compost through vermiform composting. They could use only the biodegradable waste for compost and the reject, the plastic and its management became a difficulty though it was sent to the sanitary landfill. The Company was operating for a period of eight years from 2000 to 2008.

1.12.3.1 Poabson's Agreement with the Corporation

As per the agreement the Corporation was obliged to give 300 tonnes of garbage to Poabson for making compost failing which it had to pay a compensation of 49,990 rupee a day to the company.[64] The

62 The company has several granite quarries in Kerala. It has encroached government owned property in the Ayiravalli hills through fake documents with the support of revenue officials. "Poabson Group Own Government Land in Thiruvananthapuram," *Reporter* (TV Channel), 7.00 am (12 January 2012).

63 T. C. Rajesh, "Roshathinte Idimuzhakkam…," *Kalakaumudi* 1903 (February 26, 2012): 16.

64 V. Surjith, et al., "Chavarkoonayude Arikilninnum…," *Samakalika Malayalam Varika* 5/38 (February 1, 2002): 34.

Corporation could provide an average of 200 tonnes of waste per day. In fact the plant had a capacity to process nearly 90 tonnes of garbage. Unable to keep the contract the Corporation paid a compensation of 15 crore rupees to the company.[65] The agreement also added that Poabson had to pay 2% of turnover to the Corporation.[66] However, the contract failed to mention marketing of compost manure which further became one of the other reasons that led to the withdrawal of the company from the functioning of the plant.

1.12.3.2 Problem with Marketing Compost Manure

The Corporation was marketing compost at 4.50 Rs per kilogram to the local market. This was when the same product by other companies was available even below that rate. Poabson had 3500 tonnes of compost to be marketed. Under governmental pressure Vinod Ray, the Principal Secretary of the Stores Department ordered the Government to purchase this organic manure at 4.50 Rs by a Governmental Order (G.O (Ms) No. 6/ 2002).[67] It is doubtful why Poabson, which has its own organic farming business, did not use the surplus organic manure. From this it is clear that the Company had compromised on the quality of the manure.

1.12.3.3 Strategy of Poabson

The strategy of Poabson was to be friendly with religious institutions, politicians and officials for getting local support and through them they could carry out their plans. 'Poabson could get the support of the protesting villagers by providing free building materials, influencing politicians and bribing officials, and financially helping the local churches.'[68] This proves that money and muscle power are

65 Rajesh, op. cit., 17-18.

66 "Chavar Samskarana Factorikku Anumathy Nalkuka," *Malayala Manorama* (Thiruvananthapuram), 2 December 1995, 2.

67 Shankar, op. cit., 18.

68 Interview with Jyotish, President, Koottinvathil Vishrama Kendra Samithy, Kootinvathil, 23 July 2013.

powerful tools in the hands of capitalists to betray and manipulate people's sentiments.

1.12.4 *Excel Industries*

Excel Industries, an Ahmadabad based company, was providing technical assistance to Poabson to run the solid waste treatment plant. One difficulty that Excel industries faced was that garbage was transported to the plant only after decaying. Here also the Corporation failed to provide fresh waste, the criterion for making good compost. This served as another reason for the Excel Industries to leave the plant in 2008.

1.12.5 *The Centre for Environment and Development (CED)*

The Centre for Environment and Development took charge of running the plant after Excel Industries left the plant. It was an accredited agency of the Government of Kerala for Solid Waste Management recognized by the Central Government.[69] It made a contract with the Corporation for two years, later extended for another two years. To Dr. Babu Ambat, the Executive Director, CED, the Centre could not run the plant only by accepting running charge without making profit.[70] Excel Industries left the plant in 2012; after that the Corporation took the management of running the plant which fell into evil hands leading to criticisms from all corners.

1.13 Criticism against the Plant

There were often criticisms against the functioning of the plant. The presence of non-segregated waste posed technical snags which threatened the smooth functioning of the plant. These were because of the waste contained 30-40% of plastics and other non-

69 P. K. Manoj Kumar and Hena Bahuleyan, *Statement of Facts, in Memorandum of Writ Petition Filed under Article 226 of the Constitution of India,* 1 January 2012.

70 "Vilappilsala Plantinte Nadathippu Company Ozhiyunnu," *Malayala Manorama* (Thiruvananthapuram), 8 February 2012, 2.

biodegradable matter.[71] In addition to these, the plants in Vijayawada and Vilappilsala are topographically different. The first one is situated in a plain whereas the latter is near a water source.[72] The climate in Andhra Pradesh is hot and dry whereas in Kerala it is humid and gets almost six to nine months monsoon. Moreover the stench from waste polluted the air and leachate and rain water contaminated the adjacent Meenampally Rivulet which nourishes the Karamana river. The mixing of leachate into the water threatened the health of the villagers. The Pollution Control Board also found fault with the plant.[73] At this stage people began to organize and protest which resulted in the formation of various organizations.

1.14 Various Protest Initiatives

Various initiatives of people's struggle can be categorized into two phases; the first during 1994-2002 and the second period from 2011 onwards. In the first phase the dominant action groups include the Vilappilsala Action Council, the Paura Samithy, the Karma Samithy, SEWA, the Nadar Co-ordination Council and churches, and in the second phase the dominant action groups include the Vilappilsala Janakeeya Samithy and the Samyuktha Samara Samithy.

1.14.1 *Vilappilsala Action Council (VAC)*

This was one of the first of the people's protests against the waste treatment plant.[74] It was formed under the patronage of the local MLA, representatives of panchayat and other organizations.[75] It has conducted Secretariat march (25 October 1999) in alliance with the women representatives of Thiruvananthapuram Self-Employed Women's Association (SEWA), submitted memorandums to the Chief Minister (28 November 2000 and 27 September 2001), conducted police station march (19 January 2001) in protest against

---

71 Nair, op. cit., 60.

72 Shankar, op. cit., 16.

73 Nair, op. cit., 60-61.

74 Interview with Joshy, Vilappilsala, 25 July 2013.

75 J.C. Johnson, op. cit.

the police cane charge on the previous day near the plant and a road roko on 4 December 2001.[76] The second place goes to the Paura Samithy.

1.14.2 *The Paura Samithy (PS)*

The Paura Samithy, which means citizens' forum, stood against the garbage plant. Most of the members of the PS were from CSI Kadampanad, situated around 50 meters away from the plant. They also have submitted memorandums to the Chief Minister (27 November 1994), complained to the Pollution Control Board (8 March 1996) and conducted torch bearing protest marches from Mulayara to Vilappilsala (10 April 1995) over the arrest of two active persons Robert Shobaham and J. C. Johnson. The Corporation tried to silence the PS by putting false cases against its leaders. Following a legal battle between the PS and the Corporation the Court issued five years stay to the plant. The PS met its expenses from voluntary contributions of local people.

1.14.3 *The Karma Samithy (KS)*

The Karma Samithy, meaning task force, was an initiative organized under all party leaders. All the party members are involved in it. The then president of the panchayat Sujatha Johny said that, 'the KS has no room for any politics.'[77] Its major activities include conducting a *hartaal*[78] and a protest march on 3 June 1999. It conducted a Secretariat march on 28 November 2000 and the submission of memorandums.[79]

---

76 J.C. Johnson, op. cit.

77 Ibid.

78 The word means the closing of all shops and institutions in a particular area in protest against either an unpleasant happening or against government policies and decisions. Hartaal is usually called off by political parties and communal organization as one of the forms of protest.

79 J.C. Johnson, op. cit.

1.14.4 *The Involvement of the Self Employed Women's Association (SEWA)*

The people's agitations were backed by the SEWA Office. On 5 June 1995 they conducted a protest march in front of the Secretariat against environmental pollution under the leadership of the SEWA Director, Nalini Naik. The SEWA representatives participated in the Secretariat march on 25 October 1999. Its director had participated along with political leaders in the discussions conducted at the panchayat office at the minister's chamber on 25 November 1999.[80]

1.14.5 *The Nadar Coordination Council (NCC)*

Though the Nadar Coordination Council was formed purely on a caste basis, it stood for a common cause. The most important initiative of protest of the NCC was the complaint to the District Medical Officer (DMO) about the functioning of the garbage treatment plant and the consequent pollution it created. Followed by this a five member *special team*[81] conducted an enquiry into the plant. In the reply to the NCC General Secretary Deva Prasad John, the special team confirmed the apprehensions of the people that no proper treatment of the waste was being done inside the plant by the CED.[82] This was an indicator to the people to know how negligent the waste treatment was. For that the NCC played a prominent role. Apart from this the religious institutions also played a decisive role.

---

80 J.C. Johnson, op. cit.

81 The special team consisted of the Additional DMO Dr. Mema, Medical Officer (MO) of Community Health Centre (CHC), Vilappil Dr. Satheesh Kumar, District Education and Media Officer S. Pushparaj and technical assistant Abhayan. *Enquiry Report against the Complaint Submitted by Nadar Co-Ordination Council against Vilappilsala Waste Factory*, No. E1/29/11/ CHCV, V. Susheel Kumar, Health Supervisor, Community Health Centre, Vilappil, 18 January 2011.

82 Ibid.

1.14.6 *Religious Interferences: Intervention of the CSI South Kerala Diocese*

Religious institutions like churches, temples and mosques also participated in the struggle. As the majority of Christians living near the plant belong to the CSI South Kerala Diocese, the church was forced to intervene. The response of thie church 'seems' a balanced one with a leaning towards the Corporation. It was in the midst of this contradicting position, the church reiterated that the Corporation and the government should ensure that people's fears and doubts are cleared. In this context it was the then Bishop Samuel Amritam who really intervened in the issue. His stand was well- balanced one and he expressed his concerns regarding the safety of people and demands to the District Collector, but the successive leaderships were not keen on the issue.

1.14.6.1 Role and Demands of Bishop Amritam

Bishop Amritam along with different socio- political leaders visited the plant site on 10 February 1995 and stressed the need for getting rid of the garbage treatment plant, and expressed the willingness on his part to compensate the loss of the Corporation by taking up the plot to the diocese.[83] He held that the plant was operating without addressing people's apprehensions. He was sure that more than 30,000 of people living in 5 km radius of the plant would be affected by air, land and water pollution.[84] He then convened meetings with the District Collector, Corporation officials and people's representatives in the Bishop house. After that in a letter to the District Collector the Bishop demanded the government should guarantee the promises made by the Corporation have been met.[85] His demands[86] were,

---

83 J.C. Johnson, op. cit.

84 "Mulayarayil Malinya Nikshepam Aruthu," *Malayala Manorama* (Thiruvananthapuram), 12 February 1995, 3.

85 Samuel Amritam, Bishop, CSI South Kerala Diocese, letter to the District Collector of Thiruvananthapuram, 16 June 1995.

86 Ibid.

i. The Corporation should give employment to the local people in removing, loading, unloading and selling of the compost manure.
ii. Regarding the safety of the workers, no hospital and slaughter house waste should be brought to the plant.
iii. The management of the plant should be done by a registered society on behalf of the people, for which the church can take initiative.
iv. The net profits should be shared by the Corporation, the Panchayat and the Society.
v. People who were being evicted from the plant site should be adequately resettled.

This arrangement should be agreed upon between the Society and the Corporation for a certain reasonable period of time. All these mean that such as intervention was for ensuring the safety of the people without compromising to the quality and efficiency of the plant.

1.14.6.2 The Response of the Successive Leaderships

The successive leaderships were not keen on the issue. They didnot show any remarkable interest in the issue amidst the innumerable problems in the Diocese. Later when the Vilappil panchayat president Sobhana Kumari was on hunger strike in October 2012, they were forced to intervene and advised the pastors to express their solidarity with the agitators. However, in all these occasions the CSI members, as being residents of that place, took part in the struggle even without the support of the Diocese. At the same time one cannot ignore the voice of the other denomenations. Others like the RC, the Lutheran, the Salvation Army and the Pentecostal church members were participating in the struggle.

1.14.6.3 Other Religious Initiatives

Apart from various attempts of protests from CSI SKD, there were other churches and religious organizations raised their voice against the plant from the initial stage itself. In a petition filed by

Japagnanam, a presbyter, mentions the names of other religious institutions involved in the struggle. Besides within a radius of 1.5 km, CSI churches in Kadampanad, Nedumkuzhy and Oottukuzhy, St. Martin's RC church in Chowalloor, Padavancode Muslim Jameath, the Bhadrakali temple and Srikanda Sastha temple in Chowalloor were also actively involved in the struggle during the mid 1990s.[87] When all these initiatives of protest failed to meet its objectives, people started to think of new forms of movements of protests, they gave birth to a common forum which resulted in the formation of the Vilappilsala Janakeeya Samithy.

1.14.7 *The Vilappilsala Janakeeya Samithy (VJS)*

The Vilappilsala Janakeeya Samithy, a registered movement (Reg. No. T 78/11), was formed on 9 January 2011 at Nedumkuzhy in connection with the blockade of garbage trucks. Their motto was "life is of utmost most importance than politics and denominations."[88] They believed rather in the strength of people than the leaders. This created a division within the VJS and this in fact led to the formation of the Samyuktha Samara Samithy. The VJS' nature of struggles is mentioned in ch.2.

1.14.8 *The Samyuktha Samara Samithy (SSS)*

The Samyuktha Samara Samithy was formed in the midst of the agitation headed by the then panchayat president Sobhana Kumari in 2012. It was the conglomeration of all party leaders and members. It held that, "no agitation succeeded without the support of political parties. Such political association is to influence the Government and police for immediate success of the protests."[89] Their strategy helped them to get media coverage and political influence. They hoped that only through political persuasion they could stop the plant functioning.

87 Interview with Japagnanam, Former Presbyter, CSI Kadampanad, 15 April 2013.

88 Vilappilsala Janakeeya Samithy (2012), CD- ROM.

89 Interview with Siva Kailas, op. cit.

1.15 Evaluation

Although it seems that in the first phase, four major divisions of people's organizations (VAC, PS, KS and NCC) were in the forefront of the people's struggle and were motivated by different interests, it is to be remembered that they were working towards a common interest that resulted in the closure of the garbage treatment plant. It is not sure that there was co-ordination between these people's groups except in some instances. Each group wanted to work independently and tried to show their dominance over the others in terms of their so called identity. Almost the same thing can be observed in the second phase of the struggle also.

1.16 Conclusion

Despite all interferences and protests, the Corporation ignored people's concerns and failed to meet its promises and objectives. This has led to the formation of different political and non political resistance movements against the plant. From the initial stage itself there were voices against the plant, but they were often ignored by the Corporation as well as the government. There were attempts made by the Corporation and plant operating companies to influence people as well as religious establishments with financial and material help. This could silence their voice only to a certain extent. At last they got a larger platform for resistance by forming Vilappilsala Janakeeya Samithy and all the other smaller resistance movements gradually merged into it. The study of the VJS needs more space. The VJS and its mode of operation will be studied in the next chapter.

Chapter 2

Nature of Resistance against the System of Waste Disposal

2. Introduction

In the first chapter, we have seen that the changing life style and the resultant consumerism have amplified the waste management crisis in Kerala. Thiruvananthapuram, the Kerala capital, also fell a victim of waste accumulation. The Corporation of Thiruvananthapuram sought various measures to sort out the issue and they started a garbage treatment plant in Vilappilsala, but the management of it created wide range of problems. Being unable to bear these problems people resisted the plant through the people's movement the Vilappilsala Janakeeya Samithy. The local context and the nature of the VJS' agitation need a careful study. This chapter is a study of how the plant had been operating in Vilappilsala, why it created problems and how the people resisted the plant.

2.1 Vilappil Village

Vilappil is one of the most important green and beautiful villages in Thiruvananthapuram district in Kerala and is situated 14 kms away from the heart of the city. It was constituted as a village panchayat in 1953.[90] It is bordered by the perennial Karmana River on the west on which the majority of the city people depend on for drinking water.[91] The panchayat is divided into 20 wards and the waste dump site Vilappilsala is located in the Chowalloor ward. The people of the village depend on nature and wage labour for their sustenance. (Map of Vilappil: Appendix IV).

2.1.1 *Socio-Economic Life of the People*

The people of Vilappil are the descendants of both native Keralites and those who migrated from the southern part of Tamil Nadu, especially Kanyakumari and Thirunelvcli.[92] Their history is linked with the history of Travancore. Their socio-economic life was shaped by the following factors: the cultural activities of Ayyan Kali,[93] Dr. Palpu,[94] and Kesavan Writer[95] and also Christian missionaries who stood against casteism and untouchability in Travancore, and the Land Reform Act acted as a harbinger in distributing land to the

90 Government of Kerala, Kerala State Planning Board, *Vilappil Grama Panchayat Vikasana Report, Janakeeya Asoothranam*, vol. 5 1997, 3.

91 Other borders include Thiruvananthapuram-Kattakada road on the south, the Vattiyoorkavu village panchayats on the west, Vilavoorkal and Malayinkil village panchayats on the south, and Kattakada, Poovachal, Vellanad and Aruvikkara village panchayats on the north. Ibid.

92 Burhan, President, VJS, letter to the Chief Minister of Kerala, 19 January 2011.

93 Ayyankali (1863-1941), born at Venganoor in Thiruvnanthapuram, was a social reformer who fought against the uppercaste dominance, untouchability and worked for the upliftment of dalits, especially the Pulaya community in South Travancore in Kerala. Government of Kerala, op. cit.

94 Dr. Padmanabhan Palpu (1863-1950), a native of Thiruvananthapuram, was a medical doctor by profession, a social reformer, a ledaer of Ezhava community, whose works had led to the formation of Sree Narayana Sadujana Paripalana Yogam (SNDP). Both Ayyankali and Dr. Palpu belonged to the lower caste. Ibid.

95 Kesavan Writer, a contemporary of Ayyankali and Dr. Palpu, though belonged to upper caste community, fought for untouchability in South Travancore. Ibid.

landless.[96] The diligence of the people could transform the barren and uncultivated land to a fertile place. This added a new dimension to their socio-economic life.

2.1.1.1 Social Life

The social life of the people of the village is a mixture of different religions, castes, languages and cultures. The educational institutions and knowledge system started by the Christian missionaries dating back to 1953[97] and conversion to Christianity enabled the people to question the age old practices of untouchability and casteism, and understand the dignity of life. The educational institutions, libraries, print and electronic media and all units of regional and national political parties are active in the village. All these factors mobilized the people to challenge the life threatening garbage treatment plant.

2.1.1.2 Economic Life

The majority of the villagers are daily wage labourers. Agriculture, cattle breeding and poultry farming form the subsidiary sources of income. At present agriculture has been dominated by cash crops like rubber, coconut tree and pepper. Under urbanization and the resultant competitive culture the people are leaving behind the traditional sources of sustenance, selling off their land, levelling the hills and filling the fields for residential plots for quick cash. This has pushed them to fall easy victims to consumerist culture. However, the socio-economic life has made the people politically conscious of the exploitation done in the name of the garbage treatment plant.

2.2 Historical Importance of the Plant Site

The place where the solid waste treatment plant located has a historic significance. The plant is situated in *Kanikanum Para*, which means the rock which is seen as a first sight by the Travancore king in the morning. This is the place in Vilappil where the palace could be seen

---

96 Government of Kerala, op. cit.

97 Ibid.

directly from the village.[98] Thus a historically significant place was taken by the Corporation in the name of development.

2.3 Geography of the Plant Site

The Vilappilsala Waste Treatment Plant is established in a valley where the northern and eastern steep borders are covered by natural vegetation and plantation. These slopes act as barriers for the plant which are levelled down for the construction of the plant. The steep slopes end in a small rivulet called Meenampally rivulet which finally opens into the Karamana river lying 4 km on the south-west of the plant.[99] The steep nature of the plant site and proximity to water source pose the threat of water pollution. Thus, the geographical inappropriateness of the place is responsible for environmental pollution which finally has made people turn against the plant. Furthermore the political situation has also worsened the problem.

2.4 Political Background

The plant was inaugurated at a time when the local panchayat, Corporation and the State Government administrations were headed by the Leftist party. Consequently there was consensus among all administrative levels in the matters of selection of place for the garbage treatment plant. At present the State and the local gram Panchayat administrations are in the hands of the Congress party whereas the Corporation is headed by the Communist party. This often led to tugs of war between various levels of administration and that could be one among the reasons for the conflict over the

98 The history behind this site is that the Travancore king used to visit this place on horseback as part of his pleasure trips where he would take rest and see the surrounding place as *kani*, the first sight which is considered as a symbol of good omen. Gnanadas, Deponent, *Affidavit Before the Hon'ble High Court of Kerala at Ernakulam, I. A. No. of 2012 in WP (C) No. 9 of 2012* (2 September 2012).

99 *Submitted before the Hon' ble Advocate Commission of the High Court of Kerala in WP (C) 9/2012 (A) & the Environmental Engineer of the KSPCB,* the Corporation Secretary (14 January 2012).

selection of the place as well as running of the waste disposal at the administrative level.

2.5 Waste Disposal Plant in Vilappilsala

The waste disposal plant in Vilappilsala was inaugurated on 27 July 2000.[100] It is spread over an area of 48 acres. It is an aerobic compost plant under the supervision of the Mumbai based Excel Industries, which is the pioneer in solid waste treatment through compost making. At the beginning, it was managed by the Poabson Envirotech (Pvt.) Ltd. The plant was supposed to manage the waste thrown out by a population of nearly 10 lakh people and a floating population of 2 to 3 lakh people in Thiruvananthapuram city.[101] It was supposed to process the city waste collected by the Kudumbasree Clean Well as well as Corporation sanitary workers on a 24×6 basis.[102]

2.5.1 *Waste in Vilappilsala*

Regularly more than 200 tonnes of waste was being transported to Vilappilsala in 45 trucks.[103] It was collected in the morning by the Kudumbasree Clean Well workers, and transported to Vilappilsala during night between 10.00 p.m. and 2.00 a.m. By that time the waste would have decayed. The smell produced during the transportation of waste used to make the villagers sleepless. According to H. Almitra Patel, "fresh waste is needed to make good compost. Since the decayed waste creates smell, it is better to transport it before the process of

---

100 P. K. Manoj Kumar and Hena Bahuleyan, *Statement of Facts, Memorandum of Writ Petition Filed under Article 226 of the Constitution of India* (1 January 2012).

101 *Response to Counter Affidavit Filed by Respondents 8 and 9 in WP (C) No. 9 of 2012 A* (6 February 2012).

102 Thrivikramji, op. cit.

103 "Vilappilsalayilekkkulla Malinya Neekkam Ramtam Divasavum Mudangi," *Mathrubhumi* (Thiruvananthapuram), 20 September 2011, 12.

decomposition starts."[104] 80% of the total waste reaching the plant was non-degradable and disposed of by land filling.[105]

2.5.2 *Content of Waste*

The waste collected from the city contains non-segregated waste from households, hotels and institutions, shops and markets, street sweepings, sanitation construction and slaughter houses. In 2007 the Clean Kerala Mission projected the quantity of waste produced in Kerala. The daily waste contained 49% of household biodegradable waste, 17% of waste from hotel and other establishments, 16% of plastic and rubber waste from shops and markets, 9 % of hazardous waste from street sweepings, 6% of sanitation construction waste and 3% slaughter house waste.[106]

2.5.2.1 Types of Waste Dumped in Vilappilsala

There are three types of waste coming to Vilappilsala plant.[107] They are:

i. Bio degradable waste - 114 tonnes per day on an average for composting.
ii. Non-recyclable plastic waste - 36 tonnes per day- sent to *sanitary landfill*.[108]
iii. Waste that is not easily bio-degradable - 53 tonnes per day, also sent to sanitary landfill.

---

104 Interview with H. Almitra Patel, Member, Supreme Court Drafting Committee for Solid Waste Management of Class I Cities in India, 27 October 2012.

105 *Enquiry Report against the Complaint Submitted by Nadar Co-Ordination Council against Vilappilsala Waste Factory, No. E1/29/11/CHCV,* V. Susheel Kumar, Health Supervisor, Community Health Centre, Vilappil (18 January 2011).

106 Thrivikramji, op. cit.

107 *Comments on Report of the Advocate Commission in WP (C) No. 9/2/2012*, Paras, 14 to 18.

108 A sanitary land fill is a method of waste disposal where the post waste treatment reject is covered with soil so as to avoid contamination.

This waste contains paper, dry leaves, green leaves, rotten vegetable, cotton clothes, coir stuff, husk, shells, wood and meat stall waste too.[109] It is regularly collected and dumped in the compounds of Palayam Connemara, Chalai and Manacaud markets before transporting for final disposal.

2.5.3 *System of Waste Disposal*

The system of disposal of waste follows *windrow composting*[110] and the pre and post processing rejects, and non bio-degradable materials are placed in the sanitary landfill.[111] The plant regularly receives an average of more than 200 tonnes of solid waste, which is segregated into degradable and non-degradable. For 35 days the degradable waste is stored in the yard and is ploughed once a week. The Company claims that they used to sprinkle Effective Micro Organism (EM-3) to control stink produced while ploughing. The moisture removed waste is later converted into manure by filtering using 4mm filters. The reject will be sent to land filling within the factory compound itself.[112] Later shrubs are grown over the landfills.

2.5.4 *The Claims of the Corporation*

The Corporation claims that the plant is maintaining the standard as stipulated by the MSW Managing and Handling Rules of 2000,[113]

---

109 Thrivikramji, op. cit.

110 Windrow composting is a method in compost making process where the degradable waste is put in small heaps. This is done to dry the waste so as to enable it to make compost easier.

111 *Response to Counter Affidavit Filed by Respondents 8 and 9 in WP (C) No. 9 of 2012 A,* op. cit.

112 *Enquiry Report against the Complaint Submitted by Nadar Co-Ordination Council against Vilappilsala Waste Factory, No. E1/29/11/CHCV,* op. cit.

113 The Municipal Solid Waste (MSW) Management and Handling Rules 2000, state that it is mandatory for all municipal corporations to take care of the collection, segregation, transportation and appropriate disposal of solid waste generated in the municipal area. "Malinya Samskaranam– Prasnangalum Sadhyathakalum: Janakeeya Samvadam," Thiruvananthapuram Corporation, 2013.

which state that, "land filling shall be restricted to non-biodegradable, inert waste and other waste that are not suitable either for recycling or for biological processing. Land filling should be done for the residues of waste processing facilities as well as pre-processing rejects from waste processing facilities."[114] The company could not effectively control leachate flow into the nearby water bodies and to avoid stink. This situation is the result of the negligence and mismanagement of the company which consequently led to the failure of the plant.

2.5.5 *Reasons for the Failure of Effective Management*

Despite considerable efforts made by the Corporation to improve the standard and efficiency of the plant and to achieve effectiveness in the collection and transportation of garbage to the plant since 2000, it could not attain even these minimum requirements. These led to the failure of the system of waste disposal. The major reasons for the failure of the management of waste were:

2.5.5.1 Improper Transportation of Waste

The MSW Rules 2000 state that waste should be transported in covered vehicles and the Corporation claims that they are doing so. The Corporation violated these rules and transported waste after the beginning of the decaying process, instead of specially modified vehicles they used open vehicles and rarely covered them with tarpaulin sheets.[115] This could not prevent leachate flow and stench coming out while transportation.

2.5.5.2 Ineffective Handling of Leachate Treatment Facilities

The plant became operational even before the completion of the construction of the leachate treatment plant and sanitary landfill. The plant did not have any leachate treatment facility for eight years until the Corporation took charge of managing the plant from the CED in 2008. Apart from that the directions of the Kerala State

---

114 *Comments on Report of the Advocate Commission in WP (C) No. 9/2/2012*, Para. 40.

115 Vilappilsala Janakeeya Samithy (2012), CD-ROM.

Pollution Control Board (KSPCB) and the guidelines of the Ministry of Urban Development (MoUD) were not kept in controlling the leachate flow.[116]

2.5.5.3 Piling up of Plastic Waste

The KSPCB has discovered that instead of using an incinerator plastic waste was piled up in a heap beyond limits.[117] The untreated plastic was resolved by setting fire. This has resulted in the spreading of smoke which created suffocation and asthma to the villagers. `

2.5.5.4 Lack of Increasing the Capacity of the Plant

The capacity of the plant is 90 tons per day.[118] This is insufficient to manage more than 200 tonnes of waste reaching the plant every day. This led to the dumping of waste in the plant.

2.5.5.5 Inability to Wash Vehicles Used for Transportation of Waste

Since the garbage trucks used to return to the garage only after 2 o' clock in the morning, they could not wash the vehicles daily.[119] This intensified the foul smell from vehicles. All these factors contributed to make people anti-friendly to the plant.

116 The KSPCB has found that leachate from the treatment plant as well as the land fill site flows into the Meenampally rivulet making its water unfit for human and cattle usage. *Report on Vilappilsala Bio-Waste Processing Factory, PCB/TVM- DO/CO/GEA/09* (March 18, 2011). The MoUD guidelines state that one tonne of waste would produce 200 litres of leachate. *Submitted before the Environmental Engineer of the KSPCB in WP (C) 9/2012 (A)*, the Corporation Secretary (8 April 2012).

117 *Report on Vilappilsala Bio-Waste Processing Factory, PCB/TVM- DO/CO/GEA/09*, op. cit.

118 *Comments on Report of the Environmental Engineer, KSPCB in WP (C) No. 9/2/2012* (23 January 2012).

119 *Official Note No. 2180*, Thiruvananthapuram Corporation (8 March 2012).

2.6 Vilappilsala Janakeeya Samithy (VJS)

The Vilappilsala Janakeeya Samithy is a conglomeration of all movements of people's agitation which stood against the Solid Waste Management plant in Vilappilsala. It is a movement based on people's strength for accomplishing its struggles. Though other people's movements are existing, it has got a mass appeal irrespective of religious and political differences. Under its leadership people assembled together cutting across all differences. It is the result of the past eleven years' resistance of the people against the plant. The VJS was formed on 9 January 2011.[120] They started relay fasting *satyagraha* from that day onwards. Their demand is to ensure constitutionally guaranteed rights to fresh air to breathe, clean and clear water for drinking and conditions for healthy living by closing the plant.

2.6.1 *Modus Operandi of the VJS*

The VJS is working through the people. It has a structure consisting of a patron, president, secretary and treasurer for the sake of keeping the daily log of its operation, keeping accounts, making communication with media and above all organizing people. Hence, it has become an integral part in the life of the people. The salient features of the VJS are:

a) It is self supporting, self reliant and self sufficient.
b) It has 110 units and each unit consists of 50 to 100 houses. Each family voluntarily separates a minimum amount for meeting the expenses of the struggle.[121] These grass root units will be put in the charge of leading struggles every day in rotation.
c) The VJS has alliance with other people's movements such as the struggles in Chengara, Laloor, Njeliyambra, etc. in their approaches and accepts their support.[122] At the same time

120 Marshal V. Sebastian, "Oru Gramam Sahichu, Ini Vayya," *Kalakaumudi* 1903 (February 26, 2012): 13.

121 Ibid., 14.

122 Ibid.

it is non-alliant to any political, religious and communal organizations.

d) It claims the use of the Gandhian mode of struggle and strictly wants to adhere to non- violence.[123] In the later part of the struggle, they deviate from this principle even to a minimum level.

These were the guiding principles which motivated the VJS to mobilize people.

2.6.2 *Major Struggles of the VJS*

The VJS has conducted various struggles against the Panchayat, Corporation and the Government also. They have tried various methods of struggle which include boycotting election, photo exhibitions, marches and demonstrations called *dharnas*, road blocks, blocking waste transporting trucks, hartaals, that is closing shops in protest, observing black days, hunger strikes, relay struggles, night watches and so on.

2.6.2.1 Boycotting the Election

People chose to boycott the legislative assembly election on 14 April 2011 in protest against the non-closure of the plant. Here the voting percent has come down.[124] In the words of C.R. Neelakandan, the environmental activist, 'it is only because of the non-faith of people in political parties that people abstained from election.'[125] Apart

123 "Vilappilsalakkarudethu Suddhavayuvinum Nalla Jalathinum Vendiyulla Samaram- Janakeeya Samithy," *Mathrubhumi Nattuvarthamanam* (Thiruvananthapuram), 30 January 2011, 2.

124 The voting percentage of booth No. 25 where the plant is situated was only 36.13%. Other booths in the same panchayat also showed considerable decline in the casting of votes; booth No. 20, 52.98 %, booth No. 21, 53.56%, booth No. 24, 56.25%. "Vilappilsalayil Hartaal Thudarunnu," *Mathrubhumi* (Thiruvananthapuram), 15 April 2011, 11.

125 "Vilappilsala Samaram 100 Naal Pinnittu; Perumazhayilum Avesam Jwalichu," *Mathrubhumi Nattuvarthamanam* (Thiruvananthapuram), 19 April 2011, 12.

from this they tried other forms of resistance as the panchayat office march and *dharna*.

2.6.2.2 Panchayat Office March and *Dharna*

One of the major struggles of the VJS was the March and demonstration in front of the Vilappil panchayat office on 30 April 2011. This struggle was supported by the leaders of the Chengara Struggle, Laha Gopalan and Placcimada Struggle Vilayodi Venugopal.[126] They conducted this struggle to enforce the panchayat to close the plant using the Panchayat Raj Act, but the panchayat was reluctant to do so. It was in this context the VJS had taken a decision to organize more people and to block waste carrier vehicles.

2.6.2.3 Blocking Garbage Trucks

Since the Panchayat was unwilling to close the waste treatment plant, people, under the leadership of the VJS, started blocking vehicles carrying waste from 19 September 2011 onwards. For three days the Corporation could not transport waste to Vilappilsala. It was in this context that the Government under the chairmanship of the then Chief Minister Oommen Chandy called for an urgent all party meeting which decided that gradual reduction in the quantity of waste would be considered and the plant would be closed in 11 months. The VJS gave assurance to the Government that for three months they would not block the waste carrier vehicles until 24 December 2011.[127] After three months there was no sign of reducing the quantity of waste on the part of the Corporation. Again the people started blocking waste transporting vehicles from 21 December 2011

126 L. Hari Ram, VJS News Letter (Vilappilsala: VJS, 2012), 3. The protestors were denied the right to use microphones, but it was restored followed by the blocking of the main road for about an hour. "Vilappil Panchayathinu Munnil Pradishedamirampi," *Mathrubhumi Nattuvarthamanam* (Thiruvananthapuram), 1 May 2011, 3.

127 "Vilappilsala Chavar Factory: Othutheerppine Cholli Tharkkam," *Mathrubhumi Nattuvarthamanam* (Thiruvananthapuram), 21 September 2011, 2.

onwards.[128] Being aware of the night transportation of waste and in order to prevent them they kept night vigils.

2.6.2.4 Night Vigils

Since the transportation of waste was done during nights, people used to keep night vigils.[129] This is one of the strategies which kept the people's movements alive in times of crisis. The people's agitation got the support from various sections of the society who expressed their solidarity in the form of conducting hartaals.

2.6.2.5 Hartaals[130]

The Vyapari-Vyavasayi Ekopana Samithy, a merchants' guild observed a hartaal on 12 February 2011 to express their solidarity to the Vilappilsala Janakeeya Samithy's struggles. There was a *hartaal* jointly called by the Congress party and B.J.P on 14 February 2012 over the police attack and arrest of Vilappil people on 13 February 2012.[131] Within a period of 22 months the people of Vilappil panchayat had to go through ten *hartaals*.[132] Apart from *hartaals* the people had to witness the observing of black days also.

2.6.2.6 Observing Black Days

On 24 July 2011, the VJS observed the Black Day in protest against the non- closure of the plant.[133] They raised black flags, people wore black badges and conducted a public meetings. They also conducted other forms of protests like the protest over the replacement of street lights.

---

128 Ram, op. cit., 5.

129 "Vilappilsalayilekkulla Malinyam Rantam Divasavum Mudangi," op. cit.

130 The word means closing the shops and establishments under the leadership of some political parties or communal organizations in protest.

131 "Janamunnettathil Police Pinmattam," *Mangalam* (Thiruvananthapuram), 14 February 2012, 1.

132 "Vilappil Santhiparvam," *Malayala Manorama* (Thiruvananthapuram), 18 October 2012, 4.

133 "July 24 Karidinamayi Acharikkunnu," Pamphlet, VJS, 20 July 2011.

2.6.2.7 Protest over the Replacement of Street Lights

The VJS protested over the Corporation's attempts to replace street lights with 259 set tube lights over a stretch of 5 km from Kundamanbhagam Bridge to the dump site.[134] Their protest came from the concern over accepting the generosity of the Corporation by the panchayat. Since all the forms of protests made a considerable impact on the Government, the Chief Minister himself intervened and called for an all party meeting.

2.6.2.8 Participation in the All Party Meeting

The representatives of the VJS participated in the All Party Meeting held at the CM's chamber on 1 August 2011. Though the Government did not directly give assurance of the closure of the plant, it took four major decisions. [135] They were:

i. Step by step reduction of the volume of waste in the transportation of waste.
ii. To enhance the efficiency of segregating organic waste.
iii. To speed up the construction work at Vilappilsala.
iv. To complete the construction of leachate treatment plant within a short time.

The representatives of the VJS immediately expressed their dissatisfaction over such stand of the Government and did not compromise with their demand. It was in this context the Government called for an all party meeting again at the local level as a solution to this problem, but the VJS abstained from it.

2.6.2.9 Abstaining from Discussions

The VJS, on several occasions, abstained from discussions and mediations since they felt that their demands were hardly met. The

134 "Vilappilsalayil Theruvuvilakku Sthapikkanethiyavare Nattukar Thadanju," *Mathrubhumi* (Thiruvananthapuram), 4 May 2011, 2.

135 "Vilappilsala Factory Poottanavillennu Mukhya Manthri," *Mathrubhumi* (Thiruvananthapuram), 2 August 2011, 2.

representatives kept off the meeting held on 19 September 2011 in the presence of the then Deputy Speaker of Kerala Legislature Assembly, N. Sakthan.[136] This meeting also failed to meet its end. However the Court intervened to transport the waste with police protection which the people resisted and it ended in a major struggle on 13 February 2012.

2.6.2.10 The Struggle on13 February 2012

This was one of the first major mass struggles headed by the VJS. This struggle was to prevent the transport of garbage to the plant with police protection under the Interim Order of the Kerala High Court (KHC) dated 23 January 2012 to reopen the plant after a gap of 45 days.[137] From morning 8 o'clock onwards thousands of people including women, children and old age people came to the front to lead the struggle and the struggle ended around 3.30 p.m. with the retreat of the police.

The following things happened in the struggle.

i. The police requested the people to help them obey the KHC orders, but the agitators were reluctant.[138] This led to a verbal and finally to a physical fight between the people and the police, who burst tear gas shells and resorted to cane charge and arrests to disperse the mob. The police did not even spare pregnant ladies also.[139]

136 "Vilappilsala Charchayil Janakeeya Samithy Pankeduthilla," *Mathrubhumi* (Thiruvananthapuram), 20 September 2011, 12.

137 "Four More Dumping Sites Identified," *The Hindu* (Thiruvananthapuram), 14 February 2012, 6.

138 "Vilappilsala Janaroshathil Mayor Muttumadakki," *Veekshanam* (Thiruvananthapuram), 14 February 2012, 1.

139 "Vilappilsala Pradishedam Saktham," *Mathrubhumi* (Thiruvananthapuram), 14 February 2012, 12.

ii. The agitators deployed people in three levels: children in front, physically challenged in the second place and women in the third place.[140]
iii. The VJS came in front with the slogan that they would block the garbage trucks at the cost of their lives.[141]
iv. There were minor verbal exchanges between the VJS members and Panchayat members on who would lead the struggle.[142] Finally the Panchayat members retreated from arguing and joined the agitation. This could be seen as the starting point of the conflict between the VJS and the Panchayat.
v. At noon the protestors served gruel to women under the direction of the VJS leaders to drink it slowly.[143] This was to slow down the movement of the police in arresting people.
vi. Women and children tied themselves with *saris* and *shawls* to resist the police action, and the police used knives to cut the knots to arrest them.[144]
vii. More than 500 police constables were deployed in the struggle. They used tear gas shells and grenades against the people for 19 times to contain the agitators.
viii. The police arrested 300 women including the Panchayat President Sobhana Kumari, the Samara Samithy leader Mini and beat up four leaders including the District Panchayat Member M. R. Baiju. [145]

---

140 "Vilappilsala Special Branchinu Veezhcha," *Mangalam* (Thiruvananthapuram), 14 February 2012, 5.

141 "Vilappilsala: Janakeeya Pradirodhathil Police Pinvangi," *Madhyamam* (Thiruvananthapuram), 14 February 2012, 1.

142 "People Block Transport of Garbage to Vilappilsala," *The Hindu* (Thiruvananthapuram), 14 February 2012, 1.

143 "Aadyam Kanneer Pinne Chiri," *Keralakaumudi* (Thiruvananthapuram), 14 February 2012, 2.

144 "Vilappilsla Pradisheda Kadalayi: Poleesum Janangalum Nerkkuner Ettumutti," *Keralakaumudi* (Thiruvananthapuram), 14 February 2012, 1.

145 "Aadyam Kanneer Pinne Chiri," op. cit.

ix. The major dailies reported that around 10,000 people assembled together for protest in front of the Srikanda Sastha Temple, Vilappilsala. However the Intelligence report of the police estimated that a total of 23,000 people took part in the protest.[146]

x. The District Collector imposed prohibitory orders under Cr PC 144 for a period of one week till 17 February 2012 in Vilappil Panchayat.[147] By 4.00 p.m. all the garbage trucks were brought back to the Corporation. Through this the Corporation found a temporary solution to the problem.

The Government could find consolation that they tried to implement the Court order, and the Corporation thought that it was not their fault that the garbage trucks could not be moved.[148] The Corporation took the matter to the KHC and convinced that by instituting leachate treatment machinery they could effectively manage the solid waste problem. At this juncture the KHC directed the Corporation to transport the machinery to the plant. This attempt was also foiled by the people's organization through the resistance on 3 August 2012.

2.6.2.11 The Struggle on 3 August 2012

This struggle was done against the background of the Corporation's attempts to transport leachate treatment machinery used for purifying leachate. The High Court directed the district administration to deploy 500 police personnel including 200 women constable on the struggle site to give protection for transporting the machinery

146 "Samarathinethiyavar 23000 Perennu Police Kanakku," *Mangalam* (Thiruvananthapuram), 14 February 2012, 2.

147 J. S. Jayalal, "Vilappilsalayil Nirodhananga, Hartaal," *Janayugm* (Thiruvananthapuram), 14 February 2012, 1.

148 Pradeep Malayinkeezhu, "Janakeeya Samarathinumunnil Muttumadakki Sarkarum Nagarasabhayum," *Janmabhumi* (Thiruvananthapuram), 14 February 2012, 2.

to the plant.[149] The Government authorities tried to end the struggle through negotiation from the beginning in turn without success.

These were some of the things that happened in the struggle:

i. People blocked even sub roads and made sit-ins and singing songs on roads from morning 9 o'clock onwards.[150] This was done to prevent the transport of leachate treatment machinery into the plant.
ii. Women and children were in the forefront of the struggle and they prepared *pongala,*[151] on the road. This strategy was employed to prevent the police from doing cane charge on the agitators.
iii. The agitators were arrested and brought to the nearby Govt. Upper Primary School and later released. They also joined the struggle.
iv. Miscreants destroyed and looted from private, police and fire force vehicles and pelted stones on the police.[152] Police also responded with the same. 'These were people from outside and have no connection with the agitators,' explained Rural Superintendent of Police, Thomas Kutty.[153]
v. The police was equipped with all facilities to face any situation, but restrained themselves, and finally they retreated after one and half hours of tense situation under orders from senior officials.
vi. The Kerala High Court was reviewing the situation through live videographs of the media and police videographers.

149 Manjula Chellur, Ag. CJ., & A. M. Shaffique, J., *Kerala High Court Order I. A. No. 98610 of 2012 in W.P. (C) No. 9 of 2012 (A)* (26 July 2012).

150 "Janangalumayi Yuddham Cheythu Yanthraneekkamilla: ADM," *Malayala Manorama* (Thiruvananthapuram), 4 August 2012, 2.

151 A sweet and delicious pudding, usually prepared in connection with temple festivals in Kerala as a means to appease the deity for blessing.

152 "Viplavasala," *Malayala Manorama* (Thiruvananthapuram), 4 August 2012, 2.

153 "Pinnil Aaru?" *Metro Manorama* (Thiruvananthapuram), 4 August 2012, 1.

vii. The police registered cases against 5000 agitators.[154]

The people's resistance was so strong against transporting the leachate treatment machinery to the plant amidst tight security. (i) and (iv) were the violent methods used in the struggle. The people's movement, instead of being a peace loving group, became peace breakers. Though they disclaim responsibility for the violence, they cannot completely deny moral responsibility for such untoward occurrences. This is one of the challenges that the VJS was experiencing. Since the Government was soft on people, it withdrew the police. The machinery was temporarily kept at Vilappilsala police station. In this context the Corporation decided to take the matter to the Supreme Court (SC). However the Government overcame this crisis by secretly transporting the machinery at night which again led to a grave agitation.

2.6.2.12 Struggle over Secret Transportation of Leachate Treatment Machinery

The leachate treatment equipment was transported from the police station to the plant around 2.30 a.m. on 13 October 2012.[155] Through that Government wanted to implement the Court order which could not otherwise have been done without bloodshed. The following day an indefinite *hartaal* was called off and the whole of the Panchayat joined the struggle after the declaration of an indefinite hunger strike by the Panchayat President, Sobhanakumari.

2.6.2.12.1 Mediation Efforts by the Government

The Government used the Gandhi Smarakanidhi Chairman, P. Gopinathan Nair and poet and activist B. Sugathakumari to

154 "Pradisheda Drisyangal Kodathiyilekku," *Keralakaumudi* (Thiruvananthapuram), 4 August 2012, 3.

155 "Vilappil: Rathri Nadakeeya Neekam," *Malayala Manorama* (Thiruvananthapuram), 14 October 2012, 1.

mediate between the Government and protestors.[156] Sculptor Kanayi Kunjiraman also intervened in the issue. Even mediation efforts could not move Sobhanakumari to compromise her stand. Besides, the struggle got the support of other organizations and people's representatives.

2.6.3 *Support from Other Agencies and People's Representatives*

The Federation of Residents Association of Neyyatinkara (FRAN), people's movements such as the Solidarity, the Social Unity Centre of India (SUCI) and the Kerala Swathanthra Matsya Thozhilali Federation, educationist and social activist N. A. Karim, political and social analyst B. R. P. Bhaskar, environmental and social activist Sarah Joseph, poet Sugatha Kumari also expressed their camaraderie to the agitation. However, the Corporation continued with its strategy to curb the struggle.

2.6.4 *Corporation's Attempts to Curb the Struggle*

The Corporation put false cases and made unreasonable accusations on people to put the vigour of the struggle down. They were portrayed as even extremists to suppress the spirit of the struggle.

2.6.4.1 False Charges

i. The people were diverting drainage to Meenampally rivulet.[157] It is only because of the steep nature of the topography that the leachate from the plant gets mixed with the stream. The Corporation's intention was that the factory should not be shut down at any cost.[158]
ii. The villagers were setting fire to the untreated waste in the plant.

---

156 "Mediation on to End Vilappil Stir," *The Hindu* (Thiruvananthapuram), 16 October 2012, 1.

157 "Vilappilslayile Malinya Prasnathil Ettumuttal Sakthamakunnu," op. cit.

158 "Garbage Issue Heading for Crisis," *The Hindu* (Thiruvananthapuram), 20 September 2011, 3.

iii. They manhandled the drunken garbage truck drivers posing a threat to the life of the villagers and affecting the vehicular traffic.[159]

Whether these allegations are true or not, one needs to see why such incidents occurred. All these came in the context of people's discontent over the failure of their attempts to achieve the closure of the plant.

2.6.4.2 Arrest and Release of the Leaders of the VJS

The police registered cases against 25,000 people and arrested seven villagers including the VJS' president, Burhan on 6 September 2012 on the charge of blocking garbage trucks by violating the Court order, destroying public property, looting and attacking police on 3 August 2012 struggle.[160] The people under the Aikyadardya Samity protested over the arrest in front of the Secretariat on 10 September 2012.[161] However, the arrested persons were given bail after paying 2.13 lakh rupees as a compensation for the alleged damage.[162] Here the organizational capacity and strength of the people's movement was more evident in collecting the amount for bail. 'Volunteers from each of the 110 units of the VJS collected the amount for getting bail.'[163] All the same the VJS also went through leadership issues with the Panchayat.

159 "Vilappilsala Malinya Neekam Rathriyil Thanne," *Mathrubhumi* (Thiruvananthapuram), 29 July 2011, 3.

160 "Chavar Factory Samaram: Janakeeya Samithy Nethavu Arrestil," *Malayala Manorama* (Thiruvananthapuram), 7 September 2012, 2.

161 "Emerging Keralayalla, Vendathu Jeevikkanulla Keralam: Sara Joseph," *Malayala Manorama* (Thiruvananthapuram), 11 September 2012, 2.

162 "Chavar Factory Samaram: Jamyam Kittiyavarkku Varavelppu," *Malayala Manorama* (Thiruvananthapuram), 11 September 2012, 2.

163 Interview with Sathy Kulumala, Volunteer of VJS, 9 September 2012.

2.7 Leadership Issues and the Formation of the Samyuktha Samara Samithy

In the struggle on 13 February 2012, the Panchayat political administration wanted to lead the struggle, and this led to confusion between the Panchayat administration and the VJS on who would lead the struggle.[164] This led to the formation of the Samyuktha Samara Samithy. In the struggle on 13 October 2012, the leadership issue was more obvious. Even though, Samyuktha Samara Samithy was highlighted in the media as leading the struggle, the VJS was also actively extending its support to the agitation.

2.7.1 *Samyuktha Samara Samithy (SSS)*

The Samyauktha Samara Samithy consists of the ward members of the Panchayat bearing allegiance to various political parties, under the chairpersonship of the Panchayat President. Their allegiance enabled them to get public attention through press conferences, hunger strikes, etc., which created doubts among the VJS members that they had been sidelined. The formation of the SSS was only political, though their intention was the demand for the closure of the plant. They are still continuing their relay hunger strikes at different a place, that is, the VJS at Nedumkuzhy junction and the SSS at Vilappilsala junction.

2.8 Attempts to Close the Plant

All of the people's struggles have met with their desired effect. This finally led the Government to officially declare that they would permanently close the plant. Simultaneously the Government's resolution created dissatisfaction to the Corporation and it continued with its legal battle.

164 "Attempts to Derail Protest Against Plant?," *The Hindu* (Thiruvananthapuram), 16 October 2012, 3.

2.8.1 *The Panchayat Level*

On 21 December 2010 the Congress led local Panchayat administration took a resolution to close the plant stating that the Corporation was running the plant without even getting a proper licence from the Panchayat.[165] The Panchayat Secretary has the authority to deny a licence to anything that can probably bring harm to any life form including human life, health and property under conditions as per the Kerala Panchayat Raj Act Section 232(1).[166] The Panchayat using its discretion closed the plant on 21 December 2011 with the support of the VJS.[167] Later, when the Lokayuktha ordered the Corporation to reopen the plant, the Panchayat was not ready to allow it.[168] Following this the State Government also intervened in the issue.

2.8.2 *The State Level*

On the same day as the Panchayat closed the plant, in a press conference the Chief Minister declared that the government would shift the garbage processing plant from Vilappilsala following the protest of people.[169] The Government's plan was to set up modern plants causing the least difficulty to the neighbourhood people.

Since this promise was not fully materialized, the people went with the struggle. The Supreme Court (SC) has still not given a final verdict and both the Samithies are continuing their struggle with a relay hunger strike which had lasted over five years.

165 "Vilappil Malinya Samskarana Plant Adachupoottum," *Desabhimani* (Thiruvananthapuram), 22 December 2010, 3.

166 Vasudevan Nair, op. cit.

167 "Vilappil Veedndum Yuddha Bhoomi?," *Metro Manorama* (Thiruvananthapuram), 27 July 2012, 1.

168 "Vilappilsala Factory Thurakkan Lokayuktha Utharavu," *Kerala Kaumudi* (Thiruvananthapuram), 7 January 2012, 3.

169 "Government to Shift Garbage Processing plant from Vilappilsala," http://www.keralacm.gov.in (21 December 2011).

2.9 The Present Condition of the Struggle and the Plant (2016)

On 28 February 2016 the VJS held a wide public meeting at Nedumkuzhy junction while dismantling the *samara pandal* declaring that they are withdrawing the five year long struggle in the context of the Supreme Court dismissing the review petition filed by the Corporation as the Green Tribunal and the Courts have made their judgements favouring the locals.[170] The VJS protestors have made their demands to the Government that the Corporation should hand over the property to the State Government to consider the site for implementing some people- friendly projects.[171] There are even suggestions to convert the site into prison, said N. Sakthan, Speaker, Kerala Legislature Assembly while inauguaring the 14th State Level Seminar at the Correctional Administrative Programme organised by the Department of Prisons and Correctional Services.[172] The people hope that in the nearest future they would get a blessed government project in the once accursed place.

2.10 Evaluation

The struggles of the VJS were the result of the people's suffering for over a decade. They came to the forefront of the struggle from the realization that their repeated cries, complaints and memorandums were given zero value by the respective administrative structures. Even the intervention of the administration and also the judiciary also could not satisfactorily address the people's problem. It was in this context that people went to the streets. Their methods of protest were not borrowed from any alien context; instead they evolved their own means of resistance such as resisting police arrest by tying themselves with *saris* and *shawls*, drinking gruel slowly, preparing *pongala* in the

170 "Vilappil Samaram Pinvalikkunnthayi Janakeeya Samithy," *Malayala Manorama* (Thiruvananthapuram), 28 February 2016, 2.

171 Interview with Burhan, President of Vilappilsala Janakeeya Samithy, 7 February 2016.

172 "House Prisoners in Vilappilsala: Sakthan," *The Hindu* (Thiruvananthapuram), 28 February 2016, 4.

street, etc. On seeing the genuineness of their demands, the civil society extended support to their struggle. Though the Government responded to their demands with police cases, the people did not get tired because their demand was reasonable and their strength was immeasurable.

The struggles of the VJS raise serious questions about consumer habits and the resultant waste disposal. On the one hand the city dwellers are generating waste and dumping in villages. They hardly think of appropriate alternatives apart from throwing out. On the other hand, the villagers too have similar attitudes; they also generate waste, since they have backyards unlike the city dweller, they dispose of waste either by burning or leaving it to nature. This is the 'local alternative' which they are doing. They do not want others' waste in their backyard; they enjoy all subtle consumer goods, but are not ready to show themselves as models for leading alternative life styles. In this respect the city dwellers and the villagers are not different. Even the movement people want all consumer benefits, but are not willing to sacrifice anything. They are also the victims of consumerism and have their own limitations to overcome; but one thing is obvious: their determination and strength in resisting a dominant administrative structure, which sets as a model for others, facing similar issues to unite and resist.

Conclusion

Thus we have seen that the struggle in Vilappilsala is a struggle between the powerful State and powerless people. The State has its coercive forces which can sometimes be used against the vulnerable. The Government can manipulate her power all against the poor, who have nobody to ask for their rights. She is not bothered about the pleasant cultural heritage which the villagers want to preserve. This attitude is evident in the establishment of garbage treatment in the village by the Corporation through which it challenged the identity of people and their right to have a healthy environment. The villagers hoped for a messiah, but none came. They began organizing themselves, and this in turn gave birth to a people's movement which they named the Vilappilsala Janakeeya Samithy. Afterwards, the VJS started conscientizing people. The education and above all their experiences they had helped them understand the deepening crises in their life. The support of cultural leaders, environmentalists and their association with similar movements of resistance, also enabled them to adopt the popular strategies of protests like boycotting the election, marches and *dharnas*, at the same time they developed their own methods of protests like preparing *pongalas* on the road and eating slowly to avoid or at least to delay police arrest. Their agitation did not come all of a sudden. It was the result of more than a decade long suffering. They patiently waited, sent complaints and memorandums, and finally went onto the streets. This could indeed move the Government bodies. And it could at least put a temporary relief to their affliction. Thus, the reasons for their suffering and how they fought against it, became clearer to us. However, the impacts of their suffering, their struggle and alternatives to their problem, need a closer look which will be dealt in the following chapters.

Chapter 3

Impact of the Solid Waste Treatment Plant in Vilappilsala

3. Introduction

In the second chapter we have seen the way in which people agitated against the garbage treatment plant through the Vilappilsala Janakeeya Samithy. The third chapter deals with the impact of the plant on the life of the people, the analysis and the findings. This is done with the help of questionnaires.

3.1 Impact of the Plant on the People

This part analyses how and on what extend that the people have been affected by the solid waste treatment plant. This is done with the help of analysing questionnaires.

3.1.1 *Location of the Research*

The area of study includes a radius of 3 km which involves places such as Vilappilsala, Chowalloor, Mulayara, Karunelliyod, Kuttayathukuzhy, Malayathuvila, Thinavila, Kadampanadu, Oottukuzhy, Nilamel, Kanikanumpara, Aletty, Chapatthu and Kulumala.

3.1.2 *Quantitative Method*

The researcher visited the dump site from 6 October 2013 to 23 October 2013, and distributed 150 questionnaires of which 96 people responded from a 3 km radius. 58 women and 38 men responded to the questions. These questions were mainly divided into three categories; the socio-economic life in the material base, the collective life and symbolic representation. The analysis is based on Francois Houtart Methodology of Social Analysis. The study focuses only on socio-economic factors in the material base, the role of State, civil society and people's movement in the collective life, and how religion responded to people's struggle and what ideological grounds did the Corporation and the people's movement had in the disposal of waste under the symbolic representation.

3.1.3 *Presentation of the Survey*

This survey is presented using three subtitles, the material base, collective life and symbolic representation under the Houtart Methodology of Social Analysis.

3.1.3.1 The Material Base: Socio-Economic Factors

Table 1. Gender-wise Participation.

S.No.	Gender	Frequency	Percent
1	Male	38	40
2	Female	58	60
	Total	**96**	**100**

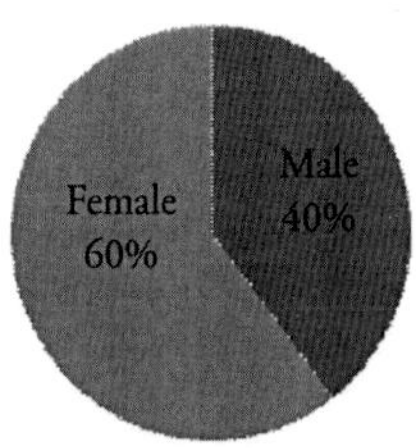

This table shows a clear picture that more women (60%) participated in the survey. Only 40% men participated in the survey.

Table 2. Age of Respondents.

S.No.	Age	Frequency	Percent
1	Below 15	4	4
2	15-20	20	21
3	21-30	24	25
4	31-40	19	20
5	41-50	23	24
6	51-60	4	4
7	61-70	2	2
	Total	**96**	**100**

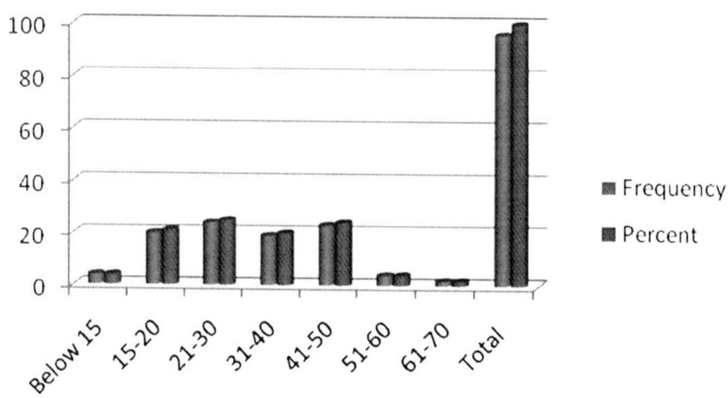

Most of the respondents were from 15-50 age group, i.e, below 15 (4%), 15-20 (21%), 21-30 (25%), 31-40 (20%), 41-50 (24%), 51-60 (4%) and 61-70 (2%).

Table 3. Distance of the Respondents from the Plant.

S.No.	Distance in meters	Frequency	Percent
1	Less than 500	14	15
2	501-1000	57	59
3	1001-1500	2	2
4	1501-2000	15	16
5	2001-2500	0	0
6	2501-3000	9	9
	Total	**96**	**100**

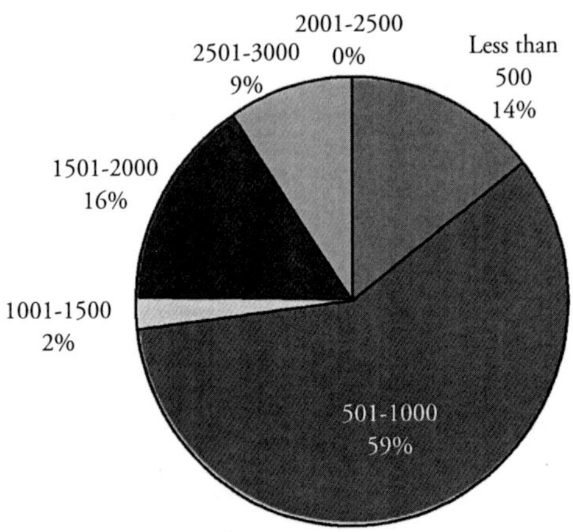

The plant became a serious threat to the life of the people within 1000m radius that is 74%. Others too had been suffering under the plant; 1501-2000m (16%) and 2001-3000m (9%).

Table 4. Occupation of the Respondents.

S.No.	Occupation of the respondents	Frequency	Percent
1	Daily wage	21	22
2	Agriculture	3	3
3	Government	7	7
4	Private	8	8
5	Others	36	38
6	Unemployed	21	22
	Total	**96**	**100**

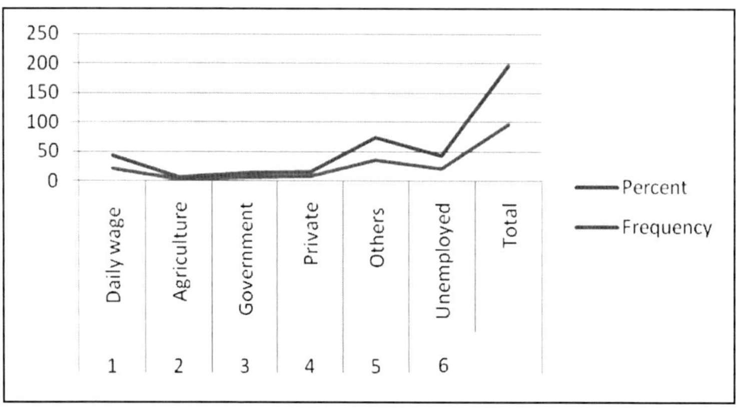

The table demonstrated the occupation of the people; Daily wage (22%), Agriculture (3%), Government service (7%), Private (8%), Others (38%) and Unemployed (22%).

Table 5. People's Reason for the Participation in the Struggle.

S.No.	Responses	Frequency	Percent
1	As it directly affected them	47	49
2	As a common problem	38	40
3	Compulsion of protestors	1	1
4	Of all reasons	6	6
5	None of the above	4	4
	Total	**96**	**100**

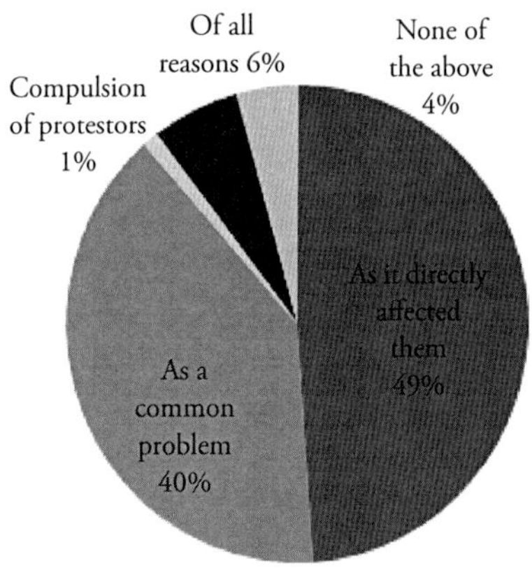

The table is an indicator to know on what reasons that the people participated in the struggle. They participated in the struggle for various reasons, such as they participated in the struggle as it directly affected them (49%), as a common problem (40%), at the compulsion of protestors (1%), of all reasons (6%) and none of the above (4%).

Table 6. Impact on Economic Life; Sale of land as its Proximity to the Plant.

S.No.	Responses	Frequency	Percent
1	Yes	26	27
2	No	70	73
	Total	**96**	**100**

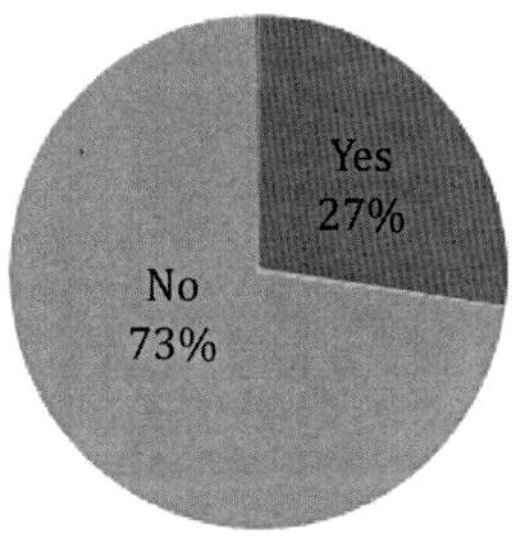

It is clear that people living nearby the plant were forced to sell their land. 27% of people sold their land, whereas 73% did not. Even though some other reasons like the situations of debts might have induced their selling, the major reason behind the selling was the health problems connected with the garbage treatment plant. In the new places also, they faced difficulty in buying houses, finding jobs and associating themselves with others. Though the others did not sell their property, they also had been severely affected by the plant.

Table 7. Loss of work on account of the Plant.

S.No.	Responses	Frequency	Percent
1	Yes	34	35
2	No	48	50
3	Can't say	14	15
	Total	**96**	**100**

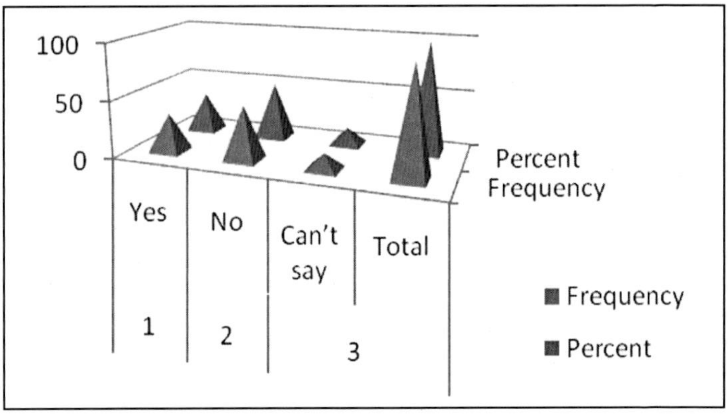

The people were daily wage labourers; one person out of three in the village, has lost his/her number of working days because of the tension created by the struggles, hartaals, road blocks, sleep followed by night vigils, fear of police action associated with the struggles, etc. Thus, redundancy had affected their daily life in meeting the family expenses and created mental tension.

Table 8. Health Impact: Frequency of Stench from the Plant.

S.No.	Responses	Frequency	Percent
1	Always	76	79
2	During the stirring of garbage	13	14
3	At the transportation of garbage trucks	3	3
4	None of the above	4	4
	Total	**96**	**100**

The stench from the garbage heap was the unbearable menace that the people have been experiencing for so long. Those who were living nearby the plant experienced the foul smell always. This means the impact of smell was so high among the people living in 1km radius.

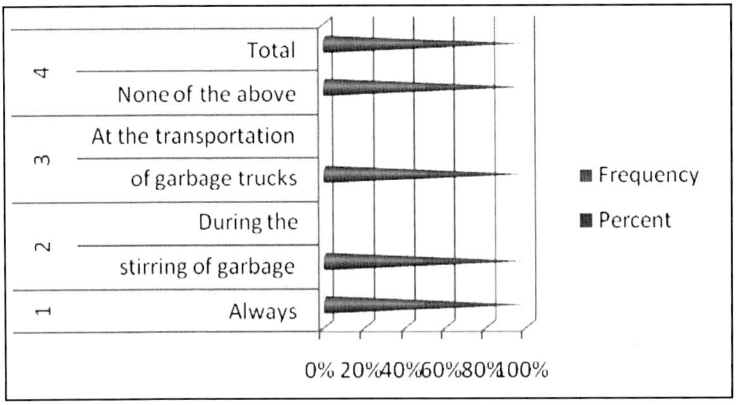

Table 9. Health Risks: Frequency of Breathing Difficulties

S. No.	Responses	Frequency	Percent
1	Always	29	30
2	Occasional	26	27
3	While stirring of waste	16	17
4	Transportation of waste	13	14
5	Can't say	12	12
	Total	**96**	**100**

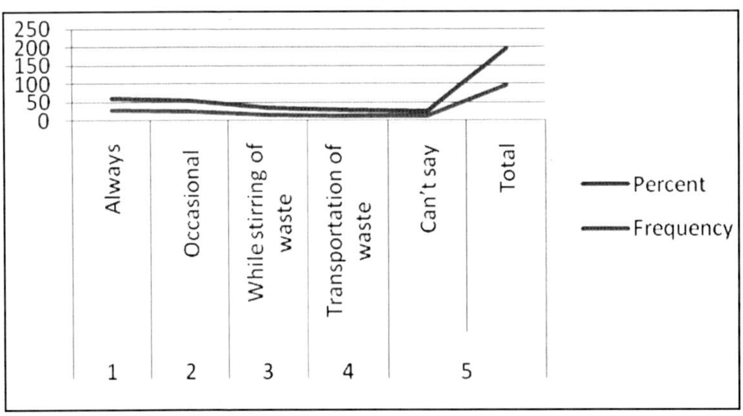

The people were forced to suffer breathing difficulties in each process of the waste management. Women, children and old age people who were always there in the houses, had to go through the severity of the situation.

Table 10. Health Problems : Frequency of Itching.

S.No.	Responses	Frequency	Percent
1	Always	30	31
2	Occasional	41	43
3	No itching	25	26
	Total	**96**	**100**

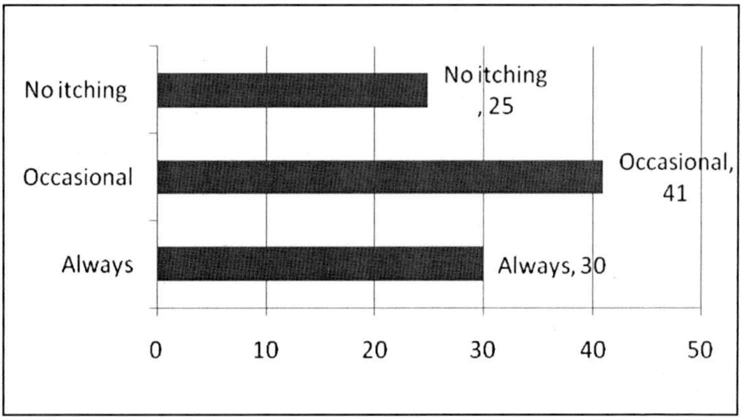

The chart shows 31% of the people have always felt itching, 43% occasionally the problem whereas 26% had no itching. The occurrence of this problem depended on the health conditions of people.

Table 11. Health Issues: Skin Disease.

S.No.	Responses	Frequency	Percent
1	Always	37	39
2	Occasional	36	37
3	Can't say	23	24
	Total	**96**	**100**

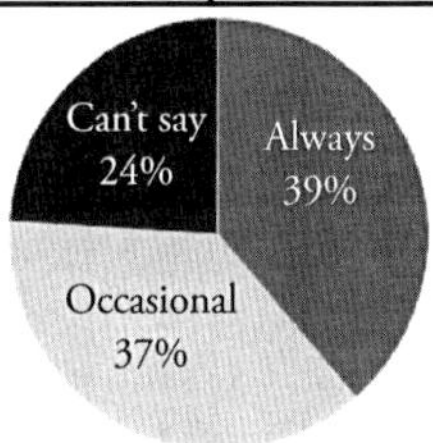

It is the infectious nature coming from the poor management of waste that created skin disease to the villagers. Besides there were problems such as diarrhoea, repeated abortions, dengue fever and ill-health of people occurred because of the plant.[173]

Table 12. Other Threats: Stray Dogs, Rodents, Flies and Birds.

S.No.	Responses	Frequency	Percent
1	Always	64	66
2	Occasional	16	17
3	Others	16	17
	Total	**96**	**100**

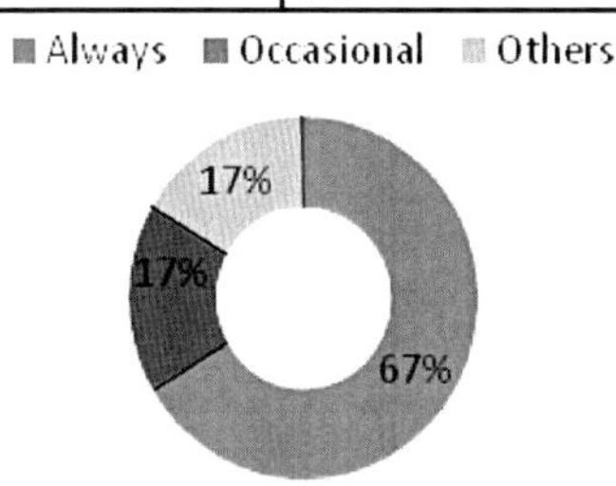

173 Interview with Shiva Kailas, op. cit.

Stray dogs from the plant posed threat a to domestic animals; rodents destroyed the agriculture and challenged people's general health, swarms of big flies disturbed their food, and birds put the residue of waste into wells and polluted drinking water and plucked crops.

Table 13. The Present Frequency of Stray Dogs, Rodents, Flies and Bird menace.

S.No.	Responses	Frequency	Percent
1	Yes	13	14
2	No	83	86
	Total	**96**	**100**

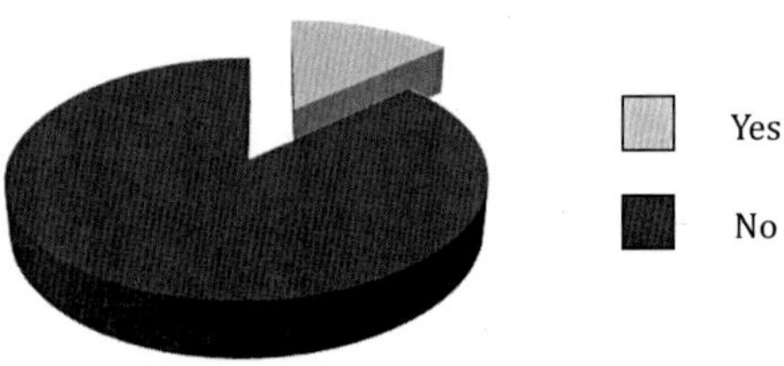

The closing of the plant almost put an end to their suffering. However the problem remains on a small level, but it would take some more months to stop it completely.

Table 14. Frequency of Water Source Utilized by Villagers.

S. No.	Responses	Frequency	Percent
1	Well	37	31
2	Rivulet	11	9
3	Well and rivulet	22	19
4	Pipe	6	5
5	All	42	36
	Total	**118**	**100**

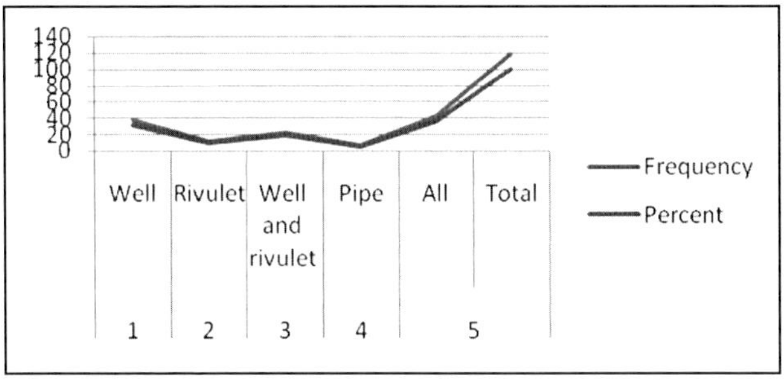

This question has 118 responses out of 96 respondents; that is, a few people recorded more than one response. It means people have been utilizing all the sources of water as this place is mainly fed by monsoon.

Table 15. Pollution of water source.

S.No.	Responses	Frequency	Percent
1	Well	5	5
2	Rivulet	17	16
3	Well and rivulet	14	13
4	Pipe	58	55
5	All the above	3	3
6	Can't say	8	8
	Total	**105**	**100**

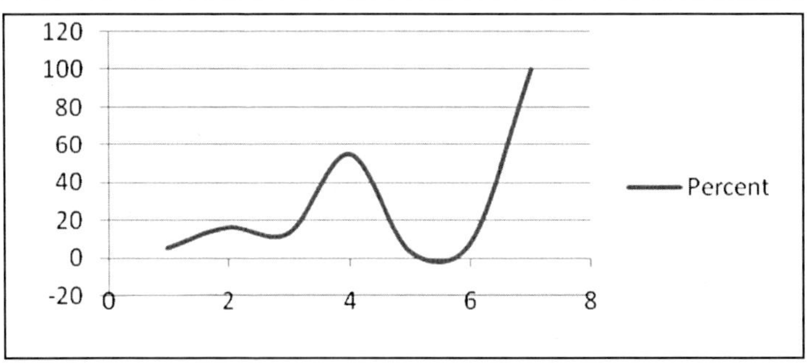

This query has 105 responses out of 96 respondents. The water was polluted because of the leachate from the plant oozing into water sources. People get pipe water from the pump house installed downstream of the Kanikanumpara rivulet.

Table 16. Failure of Marriage Proposals.

S.No.	Responses	Frequency	Percent
1	Yes	34	35
2	No	48	50
3	Can't say	14	15
	Total	**96**	**100**

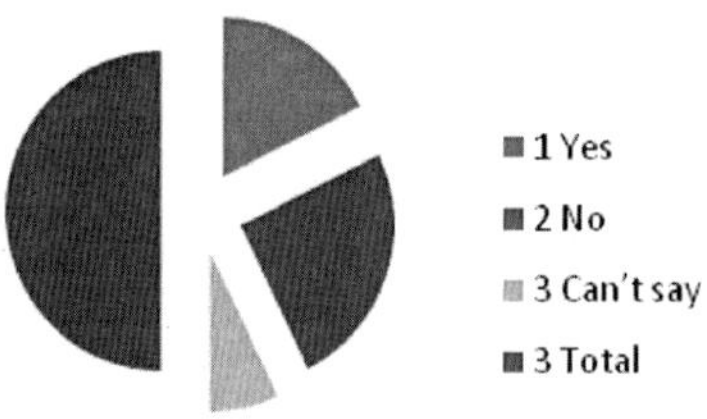

The people have experienced the failure of marriage proposals because of the bad reputation and vectors that the plant brings. We are not sure all the proposals did not take place because of the same reason, but it can be assumed that the plant is a major reason for the non fulfilment of many of the marriage proposals.

3.1.3.1.1 *Impact of the Plant on the Workers of the Plant*

The researcher interviewed[174] four people out of six workers from the same village, who were working in the garbage treatment plant. Others were from far off places and the majority of them were interstate workers. It reveals caste and labour exploitation. All of them were from the Dalit community. Women workers were doubly

174 Interviews with Sheela, 18 April 2013; Kaldharan, 11 August 2013; Asha and Das, 22 September 2013.

cheated. When the male workers were getting Rs. 240 a day, women had to be satisfied with Rs. 180 for the same job and also for the same working hours. While in work also they were not adequately protected. Even the protestors, who were also from the same village, turned hostile to the workers. Here are different responses of the people to the workers.

Table 17. Response of the Villagers to the Workers of the Plant.

S.No.	Responses	Frequency	Percent
1	Threatened and excluded them from public functions	13	14
2	Advised them to do other jobs	40	42
3	Both No.s 1 and 2	5	5
4	Behaved as usual	32	33
5	Comforted them and advised them to accept their plight	4	4
6	None of the above	2	2
	Total	**96**	**100**

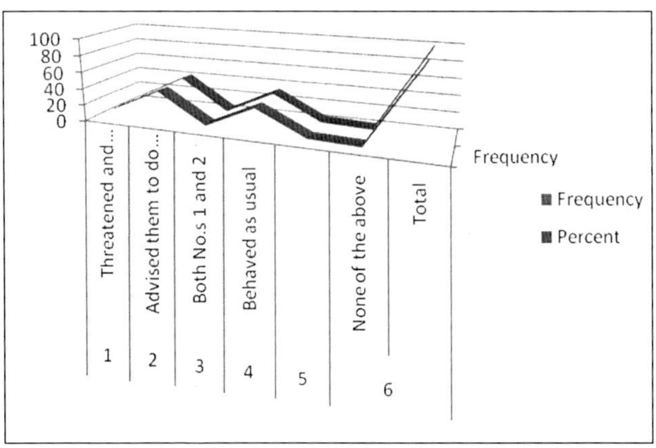

The workers in the plant were a minority community from the village itself. When we read Nos. 1& 3 together we could understand the depth of the dominance of a majority community over a minority community as shown by the responses of people altogether.

3.1.3.1.2 *Role of Women and Children*

The researcher has gone through the newspaper reports, photographs, videographs and live telecasts of the struggle. All these showed women and children were in front of the struggle. This is one of the strategies to avoid hasty police action against the protestors. This fact seems clear from the statement of the president of the VJS who says that in the past when men were deployed in front, police directly beat them.[175]

Table 18. Gender-wise Participation of People in the Struggle.

S.No.	Responses	Frequency	Percent
1	Men	2	2
2	Women	42	44
3	Equally	50	52
4	Can't say	2	2
	Total	**96**	**100**

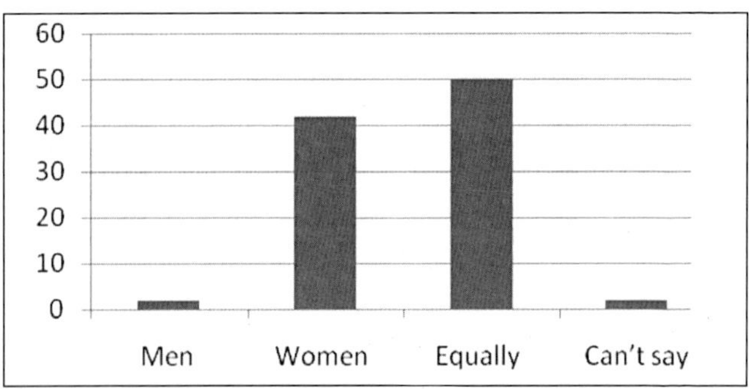

175 Interview with Burhan, President of Vilappilsala Janakeeya Samithy, Vilappilsala, 4 May 2012.

Though women were deployed in the front, an equal number of men also gave their support. It is the participation of both women and men that made the agitation a success. Moreover, the struggle for their existence was felt more by women. That was why they, in larger numbers participated in the struggle.

3.1.3.2 Collective Life

In the collective life, it includes the study of the role of the State Government, Government bodies, political parties, civil society and people's movement, etc. and how they tackled with the people's struggles in Vilappilsala.

3.1.3.2.1 *The State Government*

It was the decision of the State Government to put an end to the agitation in Vilappilsala. They tried various other places like shifting the plant to the open prison, rural areas and tea estates, granite quarries, railway platform making, land filling, but had to give up all plans following peoples' protests. It was torn between the people and the Corporation. The Government conducted repeated all-party meetings, sent mediators, imposed bans on throwing waste on roadsides, used coercive forces, etc. which all ended up in failure.[176] It was at this juncture that it took the decision to close the plant.

3.1.3.2.2 *The Corporation*

The Corporation has tried the possibilities of installing pipe compost, mobile incinerator, *bailing system*,[177] *pyrolisis*

---

176 The government tried all these options as the means to immedaiely get rid of the waste disposal crisis, but everywhere they faced strong resistance and finally they gave up all plans. This created the impasse in waste. For more details refer Appendix II.

177 Bailing is a process used to reduce the volume of waste by 1.5 m^3 by squeezing and compacting the solid waste into rectangular blocks called bails under high pressure. Jerry A. Nathanson, *Basic Environmental Technology, Water Supply, Waste Management and Pollution Control,* 5th ed. (New Delhi: PHI Learning Private Limited, 2009), 353.

gasification[178] plant in Chala market and mini plants. The pipe compost is a system of making composts using PVC pipe in the household. Till now they have installed around 70,000 pipe compost and the process is still going on.[179] The mobile incinerator had to be given up due to technical inconvenience and high maintenance cost.[180] Though the proposal was ready, the plan for pyrolysis gasification plant did not work out following the people's protest.[181] Now the Corporation is considering the possibilities of mini biogas plants in the 100 wards of the Corporation, but the construction of plants depends on the allotment of funds.[182]

3.1.3.2.3 *Judiciary*

Judicial bodies from the District Court to the Supreme Court intervened in the issue. *Lokayuktha*, the first one, had directed the Corporation to resume the work of the plant.[183] *The Ombudsman* was monitoring the functioning of the plant from 2010.[184] *The High Court* directed the Advocate Commission (AC) together with the

---

178 Pyrolisis gasification is a technology used as an alternative to incineration in which the material is treated in high temperature. It takes low or less oxygen and produces by-products that can be used as fuel. Ibid.

179 Interview with Vinod, Office Staff in Charge of Solid Waste Management, Thiruvananthapuram Corporation, 13 December 2013. Refer Appendix III, paragraph 1.

180 The incinerator was purchased at a cost of Rs. 2.5 crore through the Small Industries Development Corporation (SIDCO). "Mobile Incinerator: the Churning Sees No End," *The Hindu* (Thiruvananthapuram), 8 January 2013, 3. Refer Appendix III, paragraph 2.

181 For more details about how the people protested, refer Appendix III, paragraph 3.

182 Interview with Santhosh, JAT of Thiruvananthapuram Corporation, Thiruvananthapuram, 13 December 2013.

183 "Vilappilsala Factory Thurakkan Lokayuktha Utharavu," *Kerala Kaumudi* (Thiruvananthapuram), 7 January 2012, 3.

184 *Report Submitted Before the Hon'ble Advocate Commission of the High Court of Kerala in WP (C) 9/2012 (A) & the Environmental Engineer of the Kerala State Pollution Control Board.*

Pollution Control Board to submit separate reports for review.[185] *The Advocate Commission* found that over a long period a huge quantity of waste remained unprocessed and the plant remains non- operational.[186] *The Supreme Court* directed the Corporation to reopen the plant under police protection and to keep certain criteria such as the processing of all dumped waste, daily process of 90 tonnes of waste only, following the directions of both the High Court and the Pollution Control Board, a compulsorily daily evaluation of the performance of the plant, and source treatment of waste from hospitals and flats. [187] Now the case has been shifted to *the National Green Tribunal* and it is still going on.[188]

3.1.3.2.4 *Government Bodies: The Pollution Control Board and the Swuchitva Mission*

The Pollution Control Board, at the order of the HC, visited the plant and found that the plant has a capacity to process only 90 tonnes of waste per day; the leachate from the plant is a threat to the water source and no compound wall has been made to prevent the leachate flow.[189] It is through the Swuchitva Mission, a department of the Government through which the Government wanted to implement environmental projects. It was through this mission that the Government purchased the mobile incinerator.

---

185 The High Court had directed the Advocate Commission K. Meera and the engineer of the KSPCB to the study the impact of the plant and submit separate reports so that the court can evaluate the findings to review the situation on 17 January 2012. However following the Corporation's suit, it gave an interim report to resume the work of the plant with adequate police protection. "Vilappilsala Prasnam Parisodikkan Highcodathi Commissione Niyogichu," *Kerala Kaumudi* (Thiruvananthapuram), 10 January 2012, 3.

186 *Comments on Reports of the Advocate Commission in WP (C) No 9/2/2012,* Para.s 9 and 13.

187 "Vilappilsala Plant Thurakkam," *Kerala Kaumudi* (Thiruvananthapuram), 18 April 2012, 1.

188 "Vilappilsala Rantam Varshikathil Samaram Nadathum," *Malayala Manorama* (Thiruvananthapuram), 12 December 2012, t.2.

189 "Vilappilsala Plant Vellathinu Aapathu," *Malayala Manorama* (Thiruvananthapuram), 12 April 2012, 2.

3.1.3.2.5 *Coercive Forces*

It is essential to know how the coercive forces were used by the Government in dealing with the struggle.

Table 19. Behaviour of Police in the Struggle.

S.No.	Responses	Frequency	Percent
1	Good	42	44
2	Bad	25	26
3	Don't know	29	30
	Total	**96**	**100**

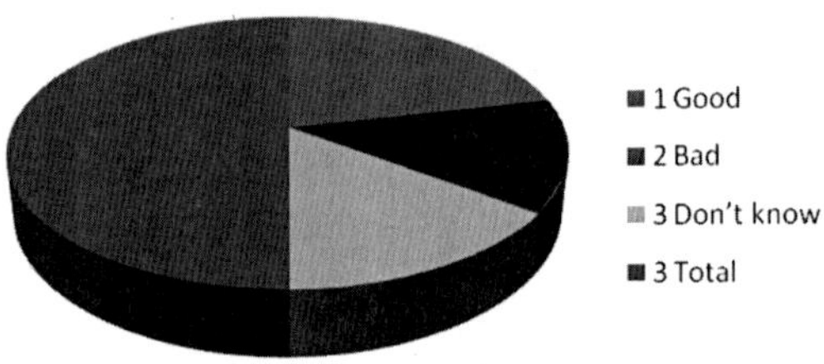

The police were instrumental in executing the interests of the Government. To them, those who stand against the Government are the adversaries. Their behaviour is convinced by only those who experience it.

Table 20. Violence Makers in the Struggle.

S. No.	Responses	Frequency	Percent
1	Police	13	14
2	Villagers	3	3
3	Outsiders	77	80
4	All of them	3	3
	Total	**96**	**100**

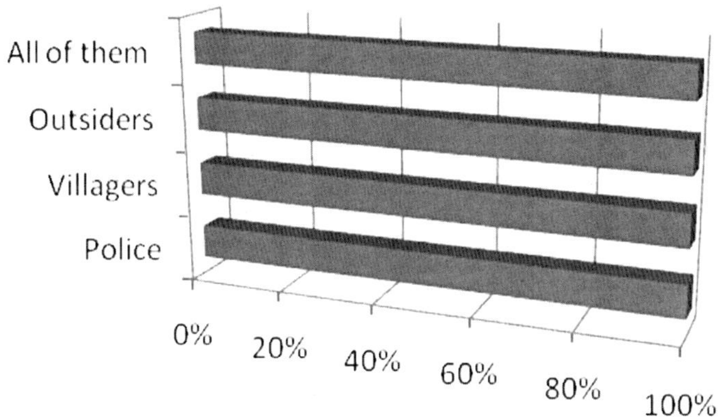

The people hold the view that outsiders were meticulously used by the Corporation and the land mafia to foil the struggle. The people whom the author had interviewed also share the same view. The author thinks the minor violence shown by villagers can be considered as part of people's resistance.

Table 21. People's Belief in Political Parties

S.No.	Responses	Frequency	Percent
1	Yes	33	34
2	No	50	52
3	Can't say	13	14
	Total	**96**	**100**

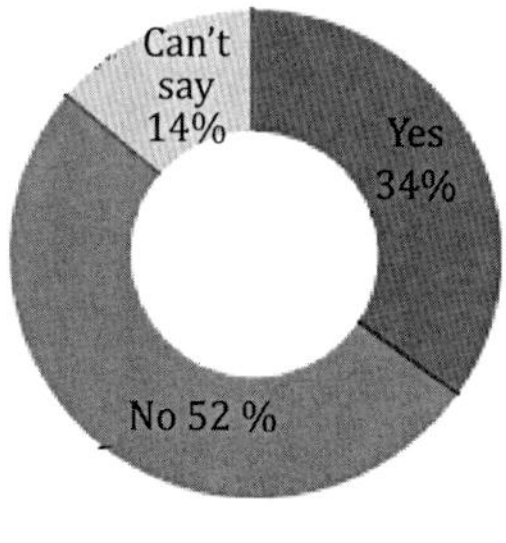

People have their own political associations, but the majority of the villagers do not believe in the capacity of any of the political parties even though the units of all political parties are active in the village.

Table 22. Media: Did the Media Give Sufficient Coverage to the Struggle?

S.No.	Response	Frequency	Percent
1	Yes	96	100
2	No	0	0
	Total	**96**	**100**

All the media including the print and visual media gave coverage to the struggle. This includes newspapers *the Malayala Manaorama, the Mathrubhumi, the Kerala Kaumudi, the Desabhimani, the Veekshanam, the Hindu, the New Indian Express, the Times of India,* etc. and T.V Channels like *the Asianet, the Surya, the India Vision, the KCN etc.* 100 percent of the people believe that their cause was given sufficient coverage in the media.

3.1.3.2.6 *People's Movements*

People's movements like the Karma Samithy, the Paura Samithy, the Vilappilsala Action Council; the SEWA, the Nadar Coordination Council, the Vilappilsala Janakeeya Samithy and the Samyuktha Samara Samithy had been actively taking up the issue, which the researcher mentioned in 1.14.

Table 23. The Credit of the Success of the Struggle.

S.No.	Responses	Frequency	Percent
1	People	90	94
2	Vilappilsala Janakeeya Samithy	4	4
3	Samyuktha Samara Samithy	0	0
4	Panchayat	0	0
5	None of the above	2	2
	Total	**96**	**100**

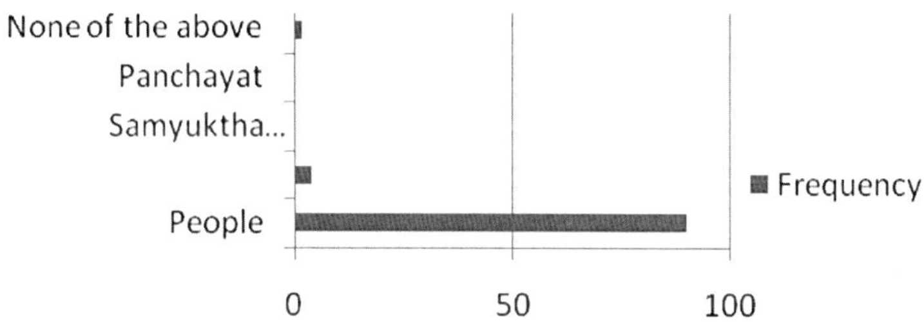

People believed that the common man has power against the powerful administration in bringing the success of the struggle. Here the role of the VJS could not be ignored. It was the VJS leading the struggle from the year 2000 onwards, whereas the SSS was formed out of a leadership struggle within the VJS. The political party leaders came to participate in the struggle on their own as members of the village or as supporters, but directions were given by the people's movement.

3.1.3.2.7 *People's Perception on the Alternative to Waste Disposal*

This section analyses people's perceptions on, the possibility of making a world with/without waste, the alternative to waste disposal, what they are doing with the waste they produce and what should the Corporation do with the waste generated within the Corporation area.

Table 24. Wasteless World Possible?

S.No.	Responses	Frequency	Percent
1	Yes	27	28
2	No	61	64
3	Can't say	8	8
	Total	**96**	**100**

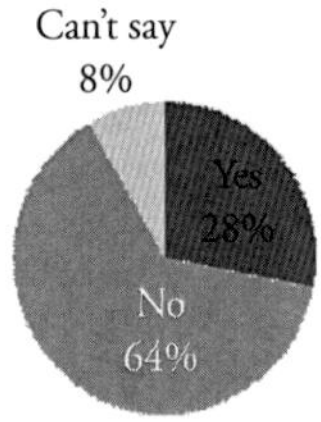

64% of the people believe that a world without waste is not possible, 28% are of the opinion that a world without waste is possible, whereas the 8% have no opinion.

Table 25. The Suitable Method for Waste Disposal in People's Perspective.

S.No.	Responses	Frequency	Percent
1	Compost making	13	12
2	Burning	15	14
3	Burying	0	0
4	Throwing out	6	5
5	Source level treatment	40	36
6	Mini plants	26	24
7	All are good	10	9
	Total	**110**	**100**

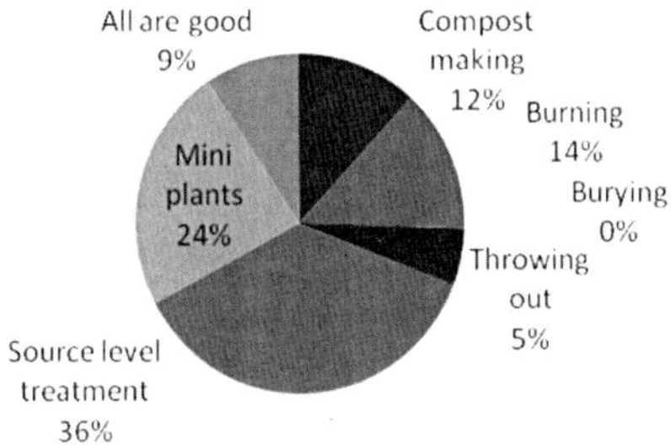

For this question multiple choices were given to the respondents to know their understandings on the suitable alternatives for waste disposal. This question has 110 responses from 96 respondents. This chart shows people's preference to different levels of waste disposal as the source level treatment, mini plants, etc.

Table 26. Household Waste Management of the Villagers.

S.No.	Responses	Frequency	Percent
1	Source level treatment	20	20
2	Compost making	32	33
3	Burying	3	3
4	Burning especially plastic	23	23
5	Throwing out	0	0
6	Doing all the above	21	21
	Total	**99**	**100**

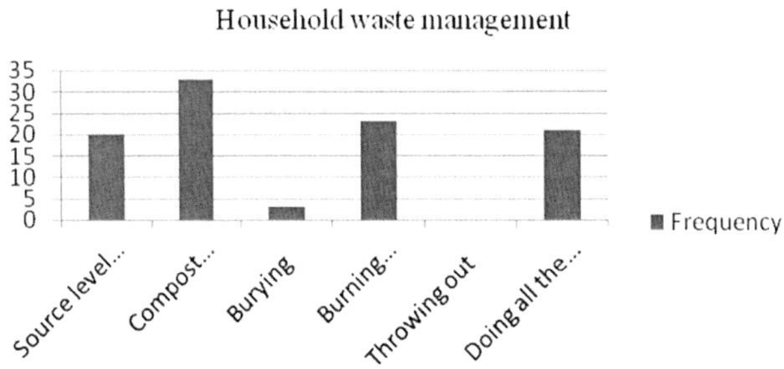

Here 99 responses were given by 96 respondents. This table shows various methods of waste disposal practiced by the people of the village. From their response it is remarkable to think that they are not throwing out their waste into others' property, but 23% of people admit that they used to burn plastic.

Table 27. The Villagers' Understanding: the Burning of Plastic produces Carcinogenic Disease?

S.No.	Responses	Frequency	Percent
1	Yes	72	75
2	No	24	25
	Total	**96**	**100**

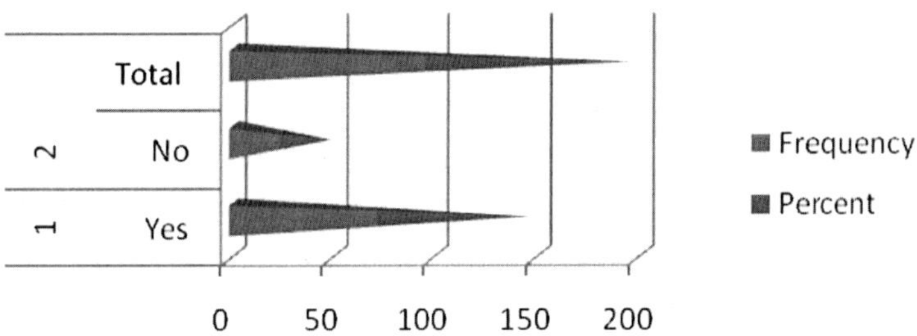

From tables 25 and 26, it is clear that people's awareness and practice are contradicting. They know that burning plastic can be harmful to health, at the same time as getting rid of plastic by burning (23%). That means they want to limit the issue of waste disposal with NIMBY syndrome. This is a typical consumerist attitude prevalent globally. Like city dwellers the villagers are not mindful of practising viable alternatives. However it is a good sign that they are trying for suitable alternatives.

Table 28. What should the Corporation do with the Waste?

S.No.	Responses	Frequency	Percent
1	Find other places for waste disposal	4	4
2	Treat waste with new machines	14	15
3	Dispose waste in Corporation's property	11	11
4	Whatever is done, no garbage should be brought to Vilappilsala.	61	64
5	None of the above	6	6
	Total	**96**	**100**

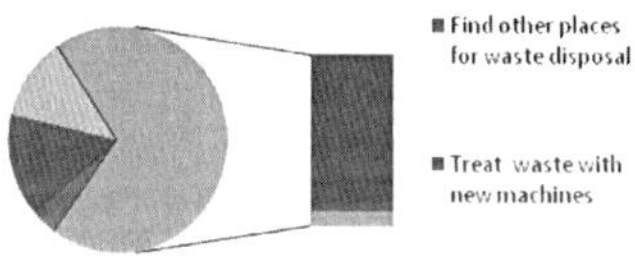

People are very conscious about their village and do not want waste in their village despite all promises of the Corporation.

Table 29. Do the Villagers Participate in the Struggle if the Factory Reopens and Functions Without Making Trouble?

S.No.	Responses	Frequency	Percent
1	Yes	66	69
2	No	9	9
3	Can't say	21	22
	Total	**96**	**100**

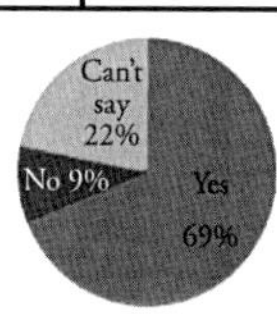

The reason why people are strongly objecting to future working of the plant even without trouble is because of the hard experiences that they had gone through.

3.1.3.3 Symbolic Representation: Religious Life

This part is regarding the participation of religious leaders and the support which the church extended to the struggle.

Table 30. Did the Church Support the Struggle?

S. No.	Responses	Frequency	Percent
1	Yes	85	89
2	No	4	4
3	Can't say	7	7
	Total	**96**	**100**

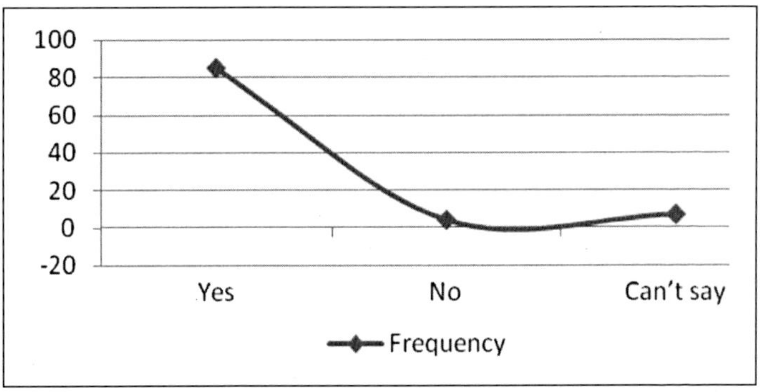

Here the local religious leaders, instead of focusing on the other worldly and telling them to accept their fate, stood with the people and critically participated in their struggle though the topmost church leaders warned the local pastors not to intervene in the issue.

3.2 Analysis of the Data

The analysis of the data reveals that all the people were living in the village either from their birth or their marriage onwards. They have no other place to live. They were doing different jobs for their sustenance. It was in this context that the garbage treatment plant came into their village betraying their right to have a clean environment. They started questioning the authorities and protesting against them to restore their fundamental rights by closing the malfunctioning waste treatment plant. People living even far from the plant also gave their active support to their issue as a common problem.

As a matter of survival issue, the plant caused problems to their existence from various dimensions including the social, economic, political, and ideological levels. Marriage proposals of youths living nearby the plant were affected because of the plant. The name Vilappilsala itself has become a synonym for dishonour and disgrace. The stench from the plant has always been a major problem to the villagers; it posed health risks like breathing difficulties, skin disease, itching, diarrhoea, abortions, etc. Stray dogs, rodents, flies and birds posed threats to their peaceful life and livestock as well. The leachate from the plant polluted their water sources on which they were depending on their domestic purposes and also on washing the cattle. All these conditions resulted in health problems which deteriorated their economic status as well.

They gradually began selling their property even at cheaper prices. There was large scale exploitation which took place in the name of the struggle. The land mafia grabbed their property within 5 km radius of the plant. Political leaders, films stars, business men and land mafia leaders began to invest in land in and around Vilappilsala under the cover of the struggle. Moreover there was widespread collection of contributions from Parassala to Kazaragod.[190] We are not sure into whose hands these entire amounts went. Continuous struggles have reduced their number of working days.

In political life, the majority of people began to realize the deception made by all mainstream political parties and hence they organized and led the struggle through the people's movement

190 Ajay Muthana, "Rashtreeyam Azhukunna Malinyapuram," *Kalakaumudi* 38/47 (October 28, 2012): 6-7.

Vilappilsala Janakeeya Samithy. Though the VJS was leading the struggle, the people consider its success as the people's victory.

One remarkable thing that happened was the support given by local religious centres and leaders especially the Christian churches. Though the dioceses of the churches were reluctant to involve the pastors in the struggle, they, more or less remained silent to the issue. It not sure whether the local church leaders became involved in the struggle out of their commitment to proclaim their solidarity with the suffering people or out of social compulsion to show that they are also standing with the people.

In the struggle women and children were deployed in front so as to avoid hasty police action against them. They challenged the authorities, who were denying them the right to have a clean and healthy environment. On the one side, one can appreciate their courage; on the other side they were shields to the men. They, including even pregnant and old women also, were put to the brim to face even police action.

The Government used the coercive forces to contain the struggle. Though they tried to be patient while the struggle was going on, they pursued the leaders of the struggle by framing false cases against them. The blame of violence, created by outside people belonging to the Corporation and land mafia, was also put on them.

For the media, the Vilappilsala issue was a coverage item. Though they brought to light the news as a 'local item,' analysis of the issue through periodicals was limited. This means they were less bothered to reach the issue to a large scale public to reflect upon how they are disposing of the waste generated from their own households.

The factory workers, who joined the working in the plant out of poverty, also had a tough time during the struggle. They had not only to bear ill treatment from the village, but also had to leave the current job and seek other opportunities. It reveals that they were oppressed in the name of caste and the economic situation.

In spite of all the struggles against an ill managed waste disposal plant, the villagers are aware that the generation of waste is an unavoidable problem. They are not throwing the waste into others' property and following their own methods of waste disposal at the source itself even though some of the methods like burning are harmful to the environment.

The villagers got a sigh of relief over the Government's decision to close the plant, but that depends on the order of the court. They are fed up with the ways in which the Corporation is behaving to them, but are ready to fight yet another struggle if the plant re-opens.

There is a tendency for political parties to highjack every struggle. One significant thing that happened in this struggle was that the people did not allow any political parties to downsize their protest. When the struggle gained momentum the political parties themselves tried to add an appendage to their resistance for electoral purposes.

3.3 Findings

i. The generation of garbage is the result of consumerist culture.

ii. Vilappilsala garbage treatment plant is a product of the NIMBY syndrome of the city dwellers.

iii. Around 200 tonnes of waste in the Thiruvananthapuram Corporation has been generated by a permanent population of around 10 lakh people and 2 lakh floating population.

iv. Since the operation of the plant came to a standstill two years ago, the city dwellers are finding their own ways for the management of waste. Most of them are doing pipe compost, others are burning. And now the Corporation is thinking of the source level treatment of waste by planting mini biogas plants in all of the 100 wards of the Corporation.

v. 35 percent of the waste is generated by the floating population.[191] They do not have any commitment to the city. Even if the Corporation starts mini biogas plants, this will remain to be a permanent problem.

vi. Plastic industry and the packaged items are worsening the waste crisis. It is up to the Central Government to contain this problem through change of policies.

191 Ajay Muthana, "Rashtreeyam Azhukunna Malinyapuram," *Kalakaumudi* 38/47 (October 28, 2012): 6-7.

vii. Business people are against the ban on plastic which the Corporation had imposed recently. Now the case is going on in the Kerala High Court.[192]
viii. Waste generation has become an indicator of one's own wealth.
ix. Generation of waste has become a part of one's culture.
x. It is the convenience loving attitude of the people which has resulted in waste generation.
xi. The primacy on 'my backyard/my city to be clean' is another factor for waste generation. This neglects the 'other' even at the cost of making it unclean.

Conclusion

The Vilappilsala is the product of the city dwellers' unbridled dependency on the throw away consumerist culture. They depend on human as well as material resources from the village; in return they dump their waste and destroy the serenity of the villages. The villages also have their own problems to deal with, but the waste situation adds an additional burden to them. The villagers, who are backward educationally, economically, culturally and also caste-wise are forced to bear the brunt of the city's garbage. Neither the urban people, nor the administration cares the impact of waste accumulation in the villages. In Vilappilsala the people have silently suffered the stench of the city waste for a long period, but in the long run they broke the silence and fought against a completely oppressive system. The administration has only one purpose that is to dump the waste into the village; the people also have a single motive that is to fight for the restoration of their fundamental right to live a healthy life in a clean environment. The administration claims that they have the legal right to dump waste in Vilappilsala as they are the owners of the dumping site; but morally they are insensitive to the cries of the people. In this context, it is important to think how the villagers are suffering and how to move towards a zero waste economy, which will be discussed in the following chapters.

---

192 Ajay Muthana, "Rashtreeyam Azhukunna Malinyapuram," *Kalakaumudi* 38/47 (October 28, 2012): 6-7.

Chapter 4

Addressing Solid Waste Accumulation and Alternatives

4. Introduction

The love of plastic, coupled with a 'convenience loving' consumerist attitude, is one of the main reasons for the complex solid waste management problem. That is why in spite of all regulations, waste is accumulating. It is in this context, that the need for a proper system of waste disposal arises. There are many methods to address the solid waste situation, all of which depend on the nature of the waste. This chapter is an attempt to study how solid waste, especially plastic, becomes a threat and how to address the accumulating garbage situation and the search for viable alternatives.

4.1 Reasons for the Blooming of Plastic Industry

Plastic came as an alternative to the wood industry with the contention that it is *eco- friendly and convenient.*[193] It is lightweight,

193 It does not require felling of trees, can preserve food items unadulterated, save energy and power consumption, for instance, if we are using iron pipes for water transportation, it means 40 percent higher loss of electrical energy

easy for purchase and transportation, and its use adds to people's style and eagerness and has become the symbol of modernisation, which the consumers prioritize. It provides an annual income of Rs. 3,500 crore to the Government treasury and brings $800 million export income.[194] Thus, from the perspective of labour and production, it contributes to 0.5 percent of India's GDP,[195] direct employment to 5,00,000 people and 1,50,000 indirectly.[196] From an eco-point of view; the flowering of this industry is anti-development. In this respect the other aspect of plastic needs to be explored.

4.2 Problems with Increasing Plastic Waste

Plastic is the major contributor of solid waste. India consumes around four million tonnes of plastic a day and its demand doubles every five years.[197] This industry poses threat to all forms of life. The plastic remains in the ground as many as 400 years, retards soil fertility, blocking water sources and kills stray animals and cattle which feed on poly bags.[198] This situation requires control of the plastic industry.

4.3 Controlling Plastic and Polymer Industry

Regulating the plastic industry through various national and international regulations and local methods of waste disposal can be of great help in solving the problem of waste accumulation. It can be done through legislation, change of life style, etc.

---

caused by corrosion and inefficiency of pumping. Proshanto Banerjee, "A Fair Hearing," *Down to Earth* 11/5 (July 31, 2002): 50.

194 A. N. Bhat, "In Defense of Plastic," *Down to Earth* 10/24 (May 15, 2002): 2.

195 "Indian Plasic Industry," http://www.india-exports.com/plastic.html (10 March 2014).

196 Bhat, op. cit.

197 Nidhi Jamwal, "Swamped," *Down to Earth* 10/21 (March 31, 2002): 34.

198 Tirtho Banerjee, "Damnable Indispensability," *Down to Earth* 6/13 (November 30, 1997): 57.

4.3.1 *International Regulation on Plastic Industry*

At the international level, the *Basel Convention*[199] exhorts the member countries to dispose of waste in an environmentally sound manner.[200] The European Union does not allow any member country to produce more plastic than they can recycle or otherwise for export, but no such regulation exists in India.[201]

4.3.2 *Regulation on Indian Plastic Industry*

The Indian plastic industry constitutes 60 percent of all Indian industry compared to the world average of 15-20 percent.[202] Various attempts have been made in India to control the plastic industry. Despite the Ranganatha Misra Committee recommended the Government to ban plastic below 100 micron thickness and to the producers to buy back the PET bottles, this remains to be materialized.[203] The new Plastic Waste Management Rules 2011 say that plastic should be a minimum of 40 microns thickness which replaced the prior law of 20 microns the success of which depends on implementation.[204] There are instances of putting a ban on plastic bags in India. The Sikkim government has put a ban on plastic bags.[205] It is the lack of political will of the Government which has resulted in the accumulation of plastic.[206] As the legislation in India favours

199 The Basel Convention is an international regulation on the Trans Boundary movement of waste from Europe to the South. It was signed in March 1989 by 115 countries. India became a signatory in March 1990. Rajat Banerji, "What a Waste," *Down to Earth* 6/9 (September 30, 1997): 40.

200 Nidhi Jamwal, "Misguided Shot," *Down to Earth* 10/24 (February 28, 2002): 45.

201 Jamwal, "Swamped"..., 37.

202 Banerjee, "A Fair Hearing," op. cit.

203 Jamwal, "Swamped", op. cit.

204 Ravleen Kaur, "Partial Ban," *Down to Earth* 19/20 (March 1-15, 2011): 21.

205 The ban on plastic in Sikkim followed the death of 27 people in a landslide caused by dumped plastic bags. "Plastic Unlimited," *Down to Earth* 9/14 (December 15, 2000): 20.

206 "Plastic Surgery," *Down to Earth* 7/9 (September 30, 1998): 5.

the big polymer industry rather than the users, the plastic ban does not reduce plastic accumulation and it grows through corruption in spite of all protests. In this context we need to think of an alternative to plastic.

4.3.3 *Finding Alternatives to Plastic*

People use to burn plastic without knowing that the fumes can do lung damage. In this context the need for alternatives to oil based petrochemical plastic arises. Reducing the use of plastic, the use of cloth bags and durable products are the options. Another way is to make plastic decomposable. Plastic can be produced from starch, a natural polymer which is biodegradable, but this is more expensive than fossil based polyethylene.[207] These compostable bags, decomposed within two months, can be promoted as alternatives to plastic.[208] The only disadvantage is the production cost being high, but this can be overcome by massive production.

4.4 Integrated Waste Management (IWM)

There is no absolute method for effective waste management. Instead an integrated approach, which means incorporating different methods for the management of waste and it can make waste management holistic and effective. It starts from collection, segregation and recycling; all of them are very composite and labour intensive processes.[209] It is used in the context of the chances of fire hazards, odours and windblown debris likely to occur from open

207 It requires 300 percent more energy than what is required for the manufacture of an equal amount of fossil fuel- based polyethylene. Its process includes the transformation of the natural polymer into lactic acid, which is chemically treated to produce plastic. Why it did not get popularity is that it is 10 times expensive than the commonly used plastic. S. Venkataraman, "It's a Bad Synthetic World," *Down to Earth* 19/3 (June 16-30, 2010): 58. Adding starch from tapioca to the real plastic can also make it bio degradable. "Plastic Go Eco-friendly," *Down to Earth* 8/7 (August 31, 1999): 52.

208 Ahir Bhairab Borthakur, "Poser on Plastic," *Down to Earth* 10/12 (November 15, 2001): 24.

209 Aman Sethi, "Waste and Wealth," *Frontline* 23/7 (April 8-21, 2006): 86.

dumps.[210] The selection of disposal methods depends on the cost and local circumstances.[211] Its success or failure relies on how we are using this method, and the change of people's mind and habit, education and conscientization and simultaneous action which are vital. The chief disposal methods under the integrated approach includes the use of four 'R's and one 'L' in the waste hierarchy; they are reduce, reuse, recycle, recover and landfill.

4.4.1 *Reduce*

The concept of waste reduction has become an ideal waste management option across the world.[212] Nature has a capacity for the assimilation of waste.[213] Waste minimization becomes relevant when waste is accumulated beyond this capacity. This is possible through the joint effort of both manufactures and consumers; producing 'durables' instead of 'disposables' and changing consumer habits.[214]

4.4.2 *Reuse*

Reusing the 'once used'/ secondary resource having utility value can slow down the production of new material through which waste accumulation can be gradually cut down. It can be practised in the household itself whether it is in the form of sharing dress among siblings or exchanging machines.[215] M. K. Gandhi's letters were

---

210 S. C. Bhatia, *Solid and Hazardous Waste Management* (Delhi: Atlantic Publishers and Distributors Pvt. Ltd.), 1.

211 S. S. Purohit, *Green Technology: An Approach for Sustainable Development* (Jodhpur: Agrobios, 2008), 610.

212 Charles A. Wentz, *Hazardous Waste Management* (New York: McGraw- Hill Book Company, 1989), 119.

213 Peter Hay, *A Companion to Environmental Thought* (Edinburgh: Edinburgh University Press, 2002), 215.

214 Changing consumer habits include carrying cotton bags for shopping, purchasing in bulk, preferring reusable packaging or non packaged items, etc. Rajiv K. Sinha and Ambuj K. Sinha, *Waste Management* (Jaipur: Ina Shree Publications, 2000), 188-189.

215 Vesilind, op. cit., 11.

written on the back of used paper.[216] To popularize this method the society's attitude to the 'fresh one' as status quo needs to change.

4.4.3 *Recycle*

40 percent of the plastic waste produced in India is non recyclable and a similar quantity of the material used is in packaging.[217] The recycling industry poses potential health risks to the workers as it uses in India open burning of circuit boards or the use of acid strips.[218] Various methods can be adopted to convert non degradable plastic into degradable ones, that is, tetra packs can be recycled into boards called ecolinks.[219] Recycled polybags, which form part of plastic waste, contain non-food grade dyes with toxins like lead and cadmium.[220] Colourful plastic toys can expose children to toxicity on chewing and sucking.[221] Recycled plastic has a shorter life span and is cheaper by 20 percent.[222] Though recycling can reduce the quantity of plastic, it can make us 'pro-industrial.'[223] Environmentalists like Bharathi Chaturvedi calls 'recycling' as 'down cycling', resulting in the production of inferior plastic.[224] Not only plastic, but also other materials like paper, glass and metals can also be recycled, but the problems recycled products face is the marketability of the products

---

216 Ramachandra Guha, *Environmentalism: A Global History* (New Delhi: Oxford University Press, 2000), 19.

217 Ruhi Khandhari, "Plastic Shakeout," *Down to Earth* 18/15 (December 16-31, 2009): 24.

218 Monali Sharma, "Shear Waste," *Down to Earth* 10/21 (June 15, 2002): 24.

219 Nidhi Jamwal, "Package Solutions," *Down to Earth* 11/14 (December 15, 2002): 24.

220 Ravi Agarwal, "Packaging Plastic Policy," *Down to Earth* 8/18 (February 15, 2000): 55.

221 Uwe Hoering, "Plasticky !" *Down to Earth* 8/13 (November 30, 1999): 57.

222 Seema Kalra, "Wasteful Profits," *Down to Earth* 3/11 (October 31, 1994): 27.

223 "The Burning Question," *Down to Earth* 7/7 (February 15, 1998): 23.

224 Alice Albina, "In the Pay of Plastic," *Down to Earth* 8/17 (January 31, 2000): 24.

as they are more expensive than virgin materials.[225] Critics like Muller prefer the avoidance of waste at the production stage to developing a giant recycling economy.[226] Recycling of plastic is inappropriate in the Indian context considering the nature of garbage as it is low in calorific value and high in content of biomass.[227]

4.4.4 *Recovery*

Recovery is the process of collecting the non-separated rejects and segregating them at centralized places. It includes two methods: resource recovery and energy recovery.[228] The first can be done through rag pickers and composting, and pyrolysis gasification and incineration are the instances of energy recovery. Recovery produces secondary materials which are inferior in quality.

4.4.4.1 The Role of Rag Pickers

Rag pickers, who survive on picking garbage, play an important role in the process of resource recovery. They can be used to collect and segregate waste material, with adequate protection to control infectious disease.[229] There are over 7,00,000 rag pickers in India. They have to face social exclusion, police atrocities and bear 'civilized' people's contempt.[230] Scrap collectors happen to be Dalits and thus are considered 'unclean,' yet the rich who make the garbage are considered 'clean.'[231] To make garbage collection effective the options are privatizing garbage collection and organizing the rag

225 P. N. Mishra, *Environment Pollution and Its Control* (New Delhi: Sumit Enterprises, 2007), 166.

226 Uwe Hoering, "The Wasted Earth," *Down to Earth* 2/22 (April 15, 1994): 32.

227 Greenhill, "Wealth from Waste," *Frontline* 10/19 (September 24, 1993): 75.

228 Sandhya Venketeswaram, "Managing Waste: Ecological, Economic and Social Dimensions," *Economic and Political Weekly* 29/45-46 (November 5-12, 1994): 2908-2909.

229 Jamwal, "Swamped"..., 35.

230 Christine Furedy, "Liquidation of Solid Waste," *Down to Earth* 4/14 (December 15, 1995): 53.

231 "Public Waste Private Enterprise," *Gobar Times Down to Earth Supplement* 2/1 (May 31, 2002): 63.

pickers.[232] But this will reduce the itinerant waste pickers' right over the collection of waste for livelihood as against the private firms' claim of waste for profit.[233] Rag picking encourages exploitation of Dalits, women and children and their cheap labour, and thus are exposing them to hazardous working conditions. This cannot be promoted in a civilized society. However, they have to be accepted and appreciated as doing ecologically and economically a worthy work.[234]

4.4.4.2 Composting

Indian garbage has 35 to 45 percent wet and 70 to 90 percent dry organic content which can be converted into organic fertilizers through composting.[235] Composting is of three types; aerobic, anaerobic and vermi composting. The first is expensive and the last, though it is cheap, requires maintaining more moisture, which is difficult to achieve. The second one is a traditional method according to which garbage is put in a pit and covered with a thin layer of soil until it forms a hillock. It will become good compost in six months.[236] The compost has good structure, porosity, aeration and moisture holding capacity.[237] It can enhance soil fertility depleted by the excessive use of chemical fertilizers.[238] It could be used as an

---

232 Anupama Katakam, "On the Scrap Heap," *Frontline* 18/15 (August 3, 2001): 89.

233 Seth Schindler, Federicho Demaria and Shashi B. Pandit, "Delhi Waste Conflict," *Economic and Political Weekly* 47/42 (October 20, 2012): 18.

234 Furedy, op. cit., 53.

235 S. C. Bhatia, *Wealth from Waste*, vol. 1 (New Delhi: Atlantic Publishers and Distributors Pvt. Ltd.), 352.

236 Iqbal Malik, "Towards a Zero-Garbage City," *Manushi* 105 (March-April, 1998): 22.

237 Jayantha Sinha, et al.,"Vermi Compost: Its Proper and Successful Application in the Cultivation of Aloe *barbadensis*," in *Pollution and Biodiversity: Biosocial Aspect,* edited by Arvind Kumar (Delhi: Daya Publishing House, 2009), 257.

238 Compost can be used to restore 21.7 million ha of saline and alkaline soil in India. Almitra H Patel, "Enriching India's Soil," *Down to Earth* 10/12 (November 15, 2001): 52-53.

effective biofertilizer, but the demand for this is very low compared to chemical fertilizers.[239] Another problem is that *leachate*[240] can pollute water sources. It must be purified and then it can be used for irrigation, cattle washing, ground water recharge, pisciculture and other activities.[241] If adequate measures are taken to contain pollution, compost making is more ecofriendly. Compost can be done at small level even at the household itself. For that needs source level separation of waste into degradable, non degradable and toxic waste. The degradable waste can be composted at the household. Or else they can be sent outside for compost and recycling.

4.4.4.3 Incineration

This is a process of converting solid waste into liquid or gaseous form at a higher temperature to reduce the volume of the waste. The advantages of this method are they can be used to produce electricity and they do not consume much space.[242] The demerits of this method are that it can emit carcinogenic and *toxic organics*[243] as dioxins and

239 The reasons for the less demand are the lack of proper awareness about the advantage of biofertilizers, indifference of people, chemical fertilizers being easy to transport, the requirement of the less quantity of chemical fertilizers, the government giving too much subsidy for chemical fertilizers. (In 2001-2002 the annual subsidy was Rs. 14000 crore), etc. K. Ramachandran and K. Sahadevan, *Malinyasamskaranam Kharamalinyangal: Prasnanagalum Pariharangalum- Oru Padhanam* (Thrissur: Current Books, 2003), 11-12.

240 'Leachate' means toxins released from toxic waste when it comes to contact with water especially during rain and giving moisture while making vermi compost. Hema Jagadeesan, "Pollution," in *Understanding Environment,* edited by Kiran B. Chhokar, Mamta Pandya and Meena Raghunathan (New Delhi: Sage Publications, 2005), 143.

241 Nidhi Jamwal, "Reeds to the Issue," *Down to Earth* 10/5 (July 31, 2001): 50.

242 Mishra, op. cit., 168.

243 Toxic organic can be formed on incomplete combustion. Dioxins and furans are produced by the combustion of chlorinated organic derived from the incineration of PVC. R. Radhakrishnan, *Bio Medical Waste Management* (New Delhi: Sumit Enterprises, 2006), 14.

furans on burning PVC.[244] The production of hydrochloric acid is also dangerous.[245] In the US it is without emission whereas in India, it is not like that and its temperature is determined by its manufacturer. At present, incineration is unsuitable in the Indian context otherwise the technology has to be modified.

4.4.4.4 Pyrolysis Gasification

This technology can be used as an alternative to incineration in which the material is treated at high temperature. Power generation is done through anaerobic decomposition of organic content and the by-products can be used as fuel.[246]

4.5 Sanitary Landfill

The rejects of all the above processes are put to sanitary landfill. The landfill has a long history of 5000 years starting from the first landfill in Knossos, Greece.[247] It is the most contaminated place as it contains leachate and other toxic chemicals which can pollute the adjacent surface and ground water system. It should be carefully handled and measures to decontaminate the site should also be taken.[248]

4.6 Need for Organizing the Community

Apart from the IWM, there are other things which also need to be done for effective waste management. At the administrative level, it is the responsibility of the Local Self Governing Bodies (LSGB) to take care of the waste disposal of respective panchayats, municipalities and corporations, which often fails because of improper planning, poor technology, poorly managed waste bins,

---

244 "Hospital Waste: Management Morass," *Down to Earth* 5/31 (May 31, 1996): 31.

245 Abhijit Mitra, *Foundation of Environmental Science* (Delhi: Narendra Publishing House, 2000), 143.

246 Nathanson, op. cit., 353.

247 Mohazareen Dastur, "Unavoidable Reality: It's Time to Think Up Novel Ways to Manage Waste," *Down to Earth* 22/5 (July 16-31, 2013): 53.

248 "A Fill of Waste," *Down to Earth* 4/20 (March 15, 1996): 24.

collection and transportation, inadequacy of funds, red tapeism, lack of commitment and community awareness etc. On seeing the context of the failure of the State in waste disposal as it is under certain structures, the question is who will take the initiative for waste management? In addition to depending purely on the State, the initiative for waste management should come from the individual itself and extend to the community level. For the community participation, civil society needs to be strengthened through conscientization which can be done by local people's movements in alliance with similar organizations at the regional and national level, NGOs, religious organizations, etc. This could provide holistic participation of the community for a zero waste society.

4.7 Evaluation

Waste accumulation in India is the result of economic liberalization and consumerism.[249] Consumerism, promoted through the advertisement industry, defines happiness in terms of the satisfaction of the accumulation of 'consumable' commodities.[250] Through consumerism we want to satisfy our ego and discard things at ease.[251] The pollutant wastes are ejected at the last stage of consumption where the energy available from the resources becomes nil leading to *entropy*.[252] To stop consumerism is to stop the free flow of the market or to achieve zero-growth, but this dependence on environmentalism or

249 Rajat Banerji, "In the Line of Fire," *Down to Earth* 4/23 (April 30, 1996): 14.

250 Debal Deb, *Beyond Developementality: Constrcuting Inclusive Freedom and Sustainability* (Delhi: Daanish Books, 2009), 83 & 368.

251 Lal B. Suresh and Ravinder. M, "Environmental Pollution: Impact on Health and Economy-an Overview Study," in *Global Environmental Issues Empirical Evidences,* edited by Lal B. Suresh (New Delhi: Serials Publications, 2010), 99.

252 'Entropy' is the second law of thermodynamics; the first law states that matter-energy can neither be created nor be destroyed but can be converted from one form to another; the second law says the more we use the source of energy, the less available it becomes. Hay, op. cit., 207-208.

sustainability has been described by the so called 'developementalists' as going back to barbarianism and misery.[253]

Waste is the product of development promoted by the capitalist economy. To fight the throw away culture basically requires a fight against capitalism. The concept of development needs to be reviewed in terms of survival economy rather than the structure of the present market economy.[254] The underdeveloped countries are under polluted. The developing countries like India are not lagging behind in the case of pollution.[255] Cleaner environment is a luxury for developed nations.

Waste belongs to the property of the owner until it is removed from the household.[256] The villages are made victims of *garbage imperialism*[257] of the urban population. There should be a shift in the attitude of people in considering villages as the dumping yards for municipal waste.[258] Civil society, too, has a role in ensuring the public accountability of the government towards the management of waste.[259]

The management of waste should become part of *sustainable sanitation*.[260] Poor environmental management will lead to poor

---

253 Deb, op. cit., 174.

254 D. K. Jha, *Environmental Studies* (Kanpur: Bhaskar Publications, 2012), 218.

255 Randhir Singh, *Contemporary Ecological Crisis: A Marxist View* (Delhi: Aakar Books, 2009), 66.

256 Poornima Chikarmane and Lakshmi Narayan, "Formalizing Livelihood: Case of Waste Pickers in Pune," *Economic and Political Weekly* 35/41 (October 7-13, 2000): 3642.

257 The term actually refers to the indiscriminate dumping of toxic waste from developed countries into developing/ underdeveloped nations. Here the reference is to the dumping of Thiruvananthapuram Corporation waste into Vilappilsala without minding the sentiments of the people. Singh, op. cit., 66.

258 "Not in My Backyard," *Economic and Political Weekly* 47/29 (July 21, 2012): 8.

259 Jha, op. cit., 218.

260 Sustainable sanitation means the sanitation system that is technically manageable, socially and politically appropriate, systematically reliable;

sanitation.[261] Consequently we need to look back into our indigenous economic living system that is economically sound and hence is suitable for sustainable development.[262]

The throwaway society emerged during the late twentieth century; it consumes all natural resources, pollutes the environment and produces toxic waste and rubbish.[263] In return we are not paying nature for the waste we dump into its lap.[264] Nature has every right to be pollution free and for that the present society has to replace the ethics of anthropocentrism with biocentrism.[265] Boston, an ecopsychologist says that caring for nature is like caring for oneself, and any violation pollutes and destroys the environment, and is self destruction.[266]

Now-a-days governments are slowly beginning to respond to this pollution as the environment is becoming an electoral issue,[267] and they chart out plans for waste management. This would only lead to the compartmentalization of the issue. Instead, we need to think of environmental management which can ultimately lead to waste

---

economically affordable and that makes the use of optimum quantum of energy resources with minimum adverse impact and recovery of useable materials; which focuses source separation of pollutants, decentralization of resources and reuse of byproducts. Zaini Ujang and Morgens Henze, eds., *Municipal Waste Water Management in Developing Countries: Principles and Engineering* (Lyngby: IWA Publishing, 2006), 11.

261 Roger J. Higgins, "Environmental Management of New Mining Option," in *Environmental Management of Solid Waste: Dredged Materials and Mine Tailings,* edited by W. Salomons and U. Forstner (Verlag: Springer, 1988), 372.

262 Suresh, op. cit., 99.

263 Singh, op. cit., 33.

264 Deb, op. cit., 67.

265 This is a view held by deep ecologists, a radical group of environmentalists, who wants to probe into the depth of the ecocrisis and to address them by changing the human-nature relationship. Bas Wielenga, *Towards an Eco-Just Society* (Bangalore: Centre for Social Action, 1999), 188.

266 Hay, op. cit., 343.

267 S. K. Agarwal, *Air Pollution* (New Delhi: A.P.H. Publishing Corporation, 2005), 293.

management. This can help an organization to fulfil its heavy burden of responsibility of the future status of the world environment.[268]

The problem of solid waste goes much beyond its disposal. This involves the resolution of many technical, administrative, economic and political problems as well.[269] In the search for alternatives blindly adopting western models would not be enough as each method will be peculiar to a particular area.[270] In this context an integrated approach with more focus on waste reduction and source level disposal can reduce the accumulation of waste to some extent.

4.8 Suggestions

i. Implementing the Extended Producer Responsibility (EPR) Scheme.[271]

ii. Introducing the take back scheme.[272]

iii. It is the lack of sufficient legislation which has resulted in the production of cheap quality of plastic in abundance.[273] In this context legislation to the *Polluter Paying Principle* (PPP)[274]

268 Kamal Vasisth, *Environmental Change* (New Delhi: Maxford Books, 2008), 7.

269 Nathanson, op. cit., 344.

270 Ravi Agarwal, "Cleansing Chronicle," *Down to Earth* 9/23 (April 30, 2001): 55.

271 The term EPR means the producer should be held responsible for the waste thrown out by consumers after use. The West has introduced this scheme. V. Sridhar, "Plastic Hazards," *Frontline* 19/11 (June 7, 2002): 39.

272 The manufacturer paying the consumers for every bottle they return. Sridhar, op. cit.

273 "Plastic Unwrapped," *Economic and Pilitical Weekly* 33/52 (December 26, 1998): 3289.

274 The PPP is the price of a *good* or service should reflect its *total cost of production*, including the cost of all resources used. Thus the use of air, water or land for the emission, discharge or storage of waste is as much the use of resources as are other labour and material inputs. It seeks to rectify the market failure by making polluters internalize the cost of use or degradation of environmental resources. Hay, op. cit., 225.

can reduce the expansion of pollution and accumulation of waste.[275]

iv. Environmental damage can be limited if the producers are held responsible for their products and their harmful consequences.[276]

v. Since the Corporations are lacking in adequate funds, incorporating the private sector for the effective management of waste is possible.[277]

vi. Adopting newer technologies for turning garbage into fuel pellets.[278]

vii. *Remote Sensing and Geographical Information System* (*GIS*)[279] could be adopted for waste disposal. This could keep garbage plants away from people's habitations.

viii. One person's waste can be used as another's resources. For that waste exchange programmes between various firms and communities can be of great help.[280]

---

275 Ruth Moore, *Man in the Environment* (New Delhi: TATA McGraw Hill Publishing Company Ltd., 1975), 150.

276 Jamwal, "Swamped"..., 38.

277 Ajit Menon, "Decentralizing the Provision of Public Services: Exonera's Efforts at Garbage Collection in Madras," *Madras Institute of Development Studies* 23/1 (January, 1993): 35.

278 The process of making fuel pellets involves drying the garbage, removing the plastic, organic and iron waste, and shredding the garbage with 10 to 15 percent moisture in a disintegrator like dried grass so as to increase the calorific value of the pellets. Pelletting is facilitated through using binders such as coal tar. Anitha Khanna, "Garbage to Gold," *Down to Earth* 2/18 (February 15, 1994): 38.

279 This is a system of selecting suitable site for waste disposal based on six criteria viz., topography, climate, surface and ground water hydrology, geology, land cover and land uses. M. Vjaya Chandran, et al., "Remote Sensing Applications in Identifying Suitable Sites for Solid Waste Disposal in Visakhapatanam, Andhra Pradesh, India," in *Environmental Engineering*, edited by Arvind Kumar and Shishir Suman Mishra (Delhi: Daya Publishing House, 2010), 10.

280 K. T. Tripathi, *Current Topics in Environment Sciences* (New Delhi: Pearl Books, 2009), 235.

ix. Optimizing one's own wants is another thing helpful in waste reduction as Gandhiji did.[281]

x. Exploring the alternative use of garbage as fish/ domestic animal feed. In countries like Nigeria, garbage has been used as fish feed.[282]

xi Source level segregation, anaerobic compost, reuse and recovery of products have to be adopted.

xii. Increasing the thickness (which can enhance rag picking) and price of plastic can minimize waste.

xii. An eco-centric and a community based participatory environmental management approach involving local government, NGOs, community based organizations (CBOs), waste pickers, citizens and other voluntary organizations in the collection, transportation and management of waste should be introduced.[283] Safeguards should be taken against the failure of CBO initiatives as they are voluntary in nature.[284]

Strengthening civil society and giving awareness to communities on the systematic method of garbage clearance and removal so that even households can take an active part in the clearance of their backyards.[285]

Conclusion

Thus we have seen that there are different methods of solid waste disposal; all of them have their own shortcomings. No system is

281 Guha, op. cit., 19-25.

282 Austin Uganwa, "Filth is Food!," *Down to Earth* 5/6 (August 15, 1996): 22.

283 Marielle Snel, "Development of Non-Government and Community-Based Organizations in Solid Waste Management Collection Scheme," *The Indian Journal of Social Work* 62/4 (October, 2001): 621; Raksha Khushalini and Rajat Banerji, "Should not Go Waste, This," *Down to Earth* 5/1 (May 31, 1996): 13.

284 Krithika Srinivasan, "Public, Private and Voluntary Agencies in Solid Waste Management: A Study in Chennai City," *Economic and Political Weekly* 41/22 (June 3, 2006): 2263.

285 Menon, op. cit., 34.

completely perfect. Each alternative system has been introduced to overcome the limitation of the other. Similarly, the waste problem cannot absolutely be wiped out, but it can be minimized and the avoidable can be avoided. It is the inevitable which requires management. We need to make waste ecofriendly, that is, biodegradable, so that it can return to nature to make it assimilate to the soil. For that society as well as technology has to play the roles of facilitators. In this situation, we need to develop not only individual but also collective environmental consciousness and thought for the future generation. There should be a radical shift in our attitude and praxis which should replace consumerist adage 'my waste is your property,' with 'my waste is my property'; replace luxury with austerity; and replace life destructive nature with life affirming. This could make our environment more sustainable.

Chapter 5

Theological Reflection on Waste Management

5. Introduction

The theology that emerges from garbage states that whatever God has created is good and holy, and nothing has been created bad and unholy. It is human action which has turned the sacred into profane and we, as stewards, have the responsibility to convert the unholy into holy and return those things back to nature. Though the concept of waste management was not explicitly articulated in the Bible as a matter of a serious concern, it is not silent on the issue of waste management. This chapter is an attempt to trace a theology of waste management. For that the author wants to take two concepts and five typologies.

5.1 The Concept of 'Good'

God desires this creation to be good; according to Hebrew psychology matter is not inherently evil and nature is not hostile to God. All things are created with the purpose of fulfilling their own special functions.[286] The good of God's work is in contrast with the chaos of which darkness is predominant.[287]

The Hebrew word for 'good' is *tob.* This adjective draws attention to an object's quality and purpose. The Beauty is the purpose and order of creation.[288] It is more closely linked with the mind and opinion of God. The scope for *tob* is broad which can be used in different contexts: "agreeable, pleasant, satisfactory, satisfying, favourable, useful, purposeful, right, beneficial, ample, pretty, well formed, fragrant, friendly, benevolent, joyous, worthy, valiant, true," etc.[289]

In the priestly tradition 'good' (Gen. 1:4) is pictured in as something which is beneficial *(wayyar' elohim ki-tob)* for man.[290] Here the declaration is not a deduction from human experience, but a divine declaration that all creation is 'good.' [291] Verse 31 says 'very good,' which means completely perfect. Good also represents harmony or totality.[292] Since everything was created good, none of

286 C.T. Fritsch, *Genesis: The Layman's Bible Commentary* (London: Bloomsbury, 1960), 26.

287 John Skinner, *A Critical Exegetical Commentary on Genesis*, 2nd ed. (Edinburgh: T & T Clark, 1994), 19.

288 Gerhard Von Rad, *Genesis: A Commentary,* translated by John H. Marks (London: SCM Press Ltd., 1961), 50.

289 H. J. Stoebe, "Good," *Theological Lexicon of the Old Testament,* translated by Mark E. Biddle, edited by Ernst Jenni and Claus Westermann, vol. 2 (Massachusetts: Henrickson Publishers, 2004), 487.

290 John H. Sailhamer, "Genesis," *The Expositior's Bible Commentary*, edited by Frank E. Gaebelein, vol. 2 (Michigan: Zondervan Publishing House, 1990), 27.

291 Richard J. Clifford, S. J. and Roland E. Murphy, O. Carm, "Genesis," *The Jerome Bible Commentary*, edited by Raymond E. Brown, Joseph A. Fitzmyer, S. J. and Roland E. Murphy, O. Carm (Bangalore: Theological Publication in India, 1990), 11.

292 U. Cassuto, *A Commentary on the Book of Genesis,* translated from the Hebrew by Israel Abrahams (Jerusalem: The Hebrew University, 1961), 59.

them posed a threat to the other and there was appreciation and recognition of each other.[293]

The Greek terms for good are *agathos*, *kalos* and *chrestos*. The Q statement of Matthew 7:11 speak of agathos as 'useful.' Luke also speaks of usefulness of the term (1:53, 12: 18-19, 16:25). 'Kalos' is used figuratively as in good fruits, good works, and good shepherd (Jn.10:11). In Paul and Deutero-Pauline literature *kalos* and *agathos* are used interchangeably (Rom. 7:18, 21).[294]

God is pre-eminently the one who is 'good' and His 'goodness' is reflected in His works (Ps. 100:5).[295] God has created human beings in His own image (Gen. 1:27), and also found Him/her 'good' along with the creation, which is a reflection of His own works. There is a purpose and quality behind every creation. It becomes waste when the creation ceases to be useful, loses its purpose and quality through which the harmony and totality of the creation is broken. Hence, the management of waste involves restoring the wholesomeness of the creation and thus making it useful not only to human beings, but also to the entire creation.

5.2 The Holiness Code

The theological reason for being holy is 'be holy for I am holy' (Lev. 11:44-45, 19:2, 20:26). Etymologically the Hebrew words *kodhesh* means 'holiness' and *kadhosh* means 'holy,' which all mean 'separateness' or 'cutting off.'[296] Holiness is connected with

293 V. J. John, *The Ecological Vision of Jesus: Nature in the Parables of Mark* (Thiruvalla and Bangalore: CSS & BTTBPSA, 2002), 58.

294 The words 'agathos' (107 times), 'kalos' (104) and 'chrestos' (7 times) are used in the NT. Agathos Mt. 16X, Mk. 4x, Lk.17x. Raymond F. Collins, "Good," *The Anchor Bible Dictionary,* edited by David Noel Freedman, vol. 2 (New York: Doubleday, 1992), 1074-1075.

295 Gordon J. Wenham, *Word Biblical Commentary*, edited by David A. Hubbard and Glenn W. Barker, vol. 1 (Texas: Word Books Publisher, 1987), 18.

296 W. T. Smith and W. J. Harrelson, "Holiness," *Dictionary of the Bible,* edited by James Hastings (Edinburgh: T & T Clark, 1963), 387.

cleanliness (Deut. 23:12, 13).[297] Purity does not mean bodily or ritualistic purity only; it involves moral and ethical quality as well (Lev. 19). The English proverb says 'cleanliness is godliness.' Holy versus common and clean versus unclean and pollution. Pollution can degrade the clean into unclean, and sanctification is needed to make the clean into holy.[298] The book of Leviticus, as part of the P source, stresses the importance of holiness and ritualistic purity. Most of the Levitical laws concerned the defilement of persons through contact with corpses or carcasses. The ritually impure has to be made holy or till that time the person shall have to stay outside the camp. Holiness requires separateness, and if someone is unholy s/he needs to undergo cleansing ceremonies to enter back to the community.[299]

Holiness depends on the proximity of a person or thing to God. The unclean people have to live outside the camp. The code of holiness provides social consciousness to the people. It has a religious colouring. The holy can enrich life where as the corrupt is seen robbing life. Justice and love are the pillars of holy life.[300] Regarding the human contribution to sanctification, all Israelites, that is, everyone has the responsibility to cleanse themselves through washing or other purification ceremonies. Moreover, cleanliness and holiness can make us whole and complete.[301] The lack of purity/ holiness can drive away people from God and community feeling. Holiness can be restored by undergoing sanctification processes. And for the management of waste both the personal and community level involvements are necessary. This can be proved with the help of certain examples such as burial of human excrement and the dead,

297 Frank E. Gaebelein, ed., *The Expositor's Bible Commentary*, vol. 3 (Michigan: Zondervan Publishing House, 1992), 141.

298 Gordon J. Wenham, *The Book of Leviticus* (Grand Rapids, MI: William B. Eerdmans Publishing Company, 1979), 19.

299 Mark F. Rooker, *The New American Commentary*, vol. 3A (Nashville: Broadman and Holman Publishers, 2000), 46-47.

300 John E. Hartley, *Word Bible Commentary*, vol. 4 (Texas: Word Books Publisher, 1992), lvi- lxiii.

301 Wenham, *The Book of Leviticus...*, 21-23.

burning, landfill, using waste as resources and resistance to the throw away culture as envisioned by Jesus.

5.3 Burial of the Night Soil and the Dead

The Israelites followed the system of burial for the disposal of human waste as well as dead bodies. They used to cover night soil with soil in the context of the scarcity of water. From an ecological point of view the burial of the dead bodies was done as a means to prevent the foul smell spreading through the air via decomposition and to control the spread of infectious disease, which the Christians continued with the contention that the tomb can be a resting place for the dead bodies until the Parousia.

5.3.1 *Burial of Human Excrement*

Each soldier camp should have appropriate toilet systems as mentioned in Deut. 23:12-14. This pericope speaks about cultic purity in the camp through humanitarian and cultic laws.[302] It reminds us that God is concerned with the cleanliness of the individual so that disease will not spread to the community. The importance to personal care and public welfare can be seen in these verses. People's holiness and their public health are connected. 'Consecrate yourselves and be holy, because I am holy' (Lev. 11:44, 45:20:7, 8; 1 Pet. 1:15-16.). The purpose of holiness is to keep us nearer to God (V.14).[303] The command to bury one's excrement did not have anything to deal with moral law. This is about ceremonial purity. By regularly doing this one should be reminded of God's holiness. Even in a person's private moments, God expects holiness and He observes us all.[304] They must

302 Joseph Blenkinsopp, "Deuteronomy," *The Jerome Bible Commentary*, edited by Raymond E. Brown, Joseph A. Fitzmyer, S.J. and Roland E. Murphy, O. Carm (Bangalore: Theological Publication in India, 1990), 105.

303 Raymond Brown, *The Message of Deuteronomy* (Leicester: InterVarsity Press, 1993), 221.

304 Jack S. Deere, "Deuteronomy," *The Bible Knowledge Commentary: Old Testament*, edited by John F. Walvoord and Roy B. Zuck (Hyderabad: Authentic, 2010), 304.

be clean unless God would withdraw from their camp.[305] The waste, that is, the excrement needs to be covered; otherwise God will be offended and turn away from people because God hates indecencies *(erwah)* among them. The soldiers need to carry spade or digging tool so as to cover the excrement.[306] Cleanliness is demanded from people, which is the criterion for worshipping God.[307] Here for personal cleanliness, a spiritual/religious colouring has been given. It is the duty of each person to look after the waste produced from their body. God did not command them to give others to take the responsibility of disposing their waste. Here we could see both the individual and community level participation in the disposal of waste. This pericope could be seen as an instance of source level treatment of their waste.

This passage speaks about the traditional method of disposal of human waste. Covering the 'night soil' with soil is a method to return the waste to nature. Nature has a capacity to decompose such a waste; for that, human participation is needed, that is, the act of 'covering.' Devoid of such an act, the face of the earth is polluted. Through 'covering' we are participating in the divine purpose of keeping the mother earth *tob* and *kadhosh* or *agathos*. This process provides a cue to making compost out of human excrement.

Human waste contains two things; urine and excrement. Urine contains nutrients and can be used immediately, whereas the excreta, though rich in soil nutrients, contains pathogens and needs to be composted at least 12 months before the pathogens die off. [308] Urine

---

305 S. R. Driver, *A Critical and Exegetical Commentary on Deuteronomy*, 3rd ed. (Edinburgh: T & T Clark, 1996), 263.

306 Eugene H. Merrill, *The New American Commentary,* vol. 4 (Dallas: Broadman and Holman Publishers, 1994), 310. Each person should have a trammel. Peter C. Craigie, *The Book of Deuteronomy* (Grand Rapids, MI: William B. Eerdmans Publishing Company, 1976), 299.

307 Ex. 19:10-11, 30:18-21, Josh. 3:5, Ps. 51:7, 10. Frank E. Gaebelein, ed., *The Expositor's Bible Commentary*, vol. 3 (Michigan: Zondervan Publishing House, 1992), 141.

308 One gram of faeces contains 1,00,00,000 viruses, 10,00,000 bacteria, 1,000 parasitic cysts and 100 parasitic eggs. "We Need to Talk about Toilets," *New Internationalist* 414 (August, 2008): 8-9.

and faeces need to be separated for making compost; otherwise uria decomposes to ammonia and stinks. If urine mixes with excreta, it can pollute the ground water as well.[309] Urine, after separate treatment, can be used for agricultural purposes.[310] This is ecological sanitation or eco-sans which works on the principle of not mixing faeces, urine and water. The wet nature of human waste can be minimized by adding ash or saw dust.[311] In Deut. 23:12-14 the wet human waste was dried by putting soil over it. Through that they were also participating in ecosanitation. Here the principle of my waste, my property and my responsibility can be seen.

5.3.2 *Burial of the Dead*

In the Jewish culture, the deceased are buried as soon as possible in keeping with the tradition of ancient Israel before the kingdom of Israel came into being. They preserved the secondary burial system also, that is the reburial of the bones after the decaying of the flesh. In the second burial, the bones of the diseased persons in the family were buried collectively. This is revealed by the phrase, "to be gathered to one's fathers," (e.g., 2 Kin. 22:20).[312] Though it has a theological significance regarding the promise of God, the collective burying could be an example of managing waste through limiting space.

---

309 "What about Us," *New Internationalist* 414 (August, 2008): 20. Urine is odourless, but when it mixes with water or bacterial function takes place, it produces a foul smell. Bharat Lal Seth, "Break the Odour," *Down to Earth* 18/21 (March 16-31, 2010): 9. A person can produce 4.56 kg of nitrogen (N), 0.55 kg phosphorous (P) and 1.28 kg of potassium (K) in a year. It can rejuvenate a 200-400 sq m patch. A billion can produce six million tonnes of NPK which is one-third of the total fertilizer usage in India. "The Morning After," *Down to Earth* 17/16 (January 1-15, 2009): 47.

310 Kullon village in Sweden stores urine in separate tanks for about six months and afterwards uses it for agriculture. R. K. Srinivasan, "Urine is No Waste, "*Down to Earth* 14/11 (October 31, 2005): 46.

311 "The Flush Toilet is Ecologically Mindless," *Down to Earth* 10/19 (February 28, 2002): 37.

312 B. R. McCane, "Burial Practices, Jewish," *Dictionary of New Testament Practices,* edited by Craig A. Evans and Stanley E. Porter (Illinois: InterVarsity Press, 2000), 172-173.

5.4 Burning

Burning is a method of the reduction of the volume of waste by putting it in fire the process of which releases heat, smoke and ash residues. It was done in the context of the accumulation of waste thereby reducing its volume to the optimum level. The Jews practised burning of carcasses and wood as the methods of waste management.

5.4.1 *Burning of Carcasses after Sacrifices*

The Israelites had an effective system of disposal of the carcasses left over after sacrifices. The carcasses were disposed of in two ways; one was burning and the other was to use them as food for priests. In the sacrifices meant for priests, the carcasses could be taken outside the camp and disposed of by burning in wood (Lev. 4:12). The animal remains in the sacrifices meant for leaders and ordinary persons, could be eaten by priests in a holy place (Lev. 4:26, 31, 35).[313] This was an effective way of managing such a waste.

5.4.2 *Smoke*

Smoke was presented in the Bible variously as symbols of evil,[314] destruction,[315] suffering,[316] wrath,[317] God's mercy,[318] purity or

---

313 F. Duane Lindsey, "Deuteronomy," *The Word Bible Commentary: Old Testament,* edited by John F. Walvoord and Roy B. Zuck (Hyderabad: Authentic, 2010), 181.

314 Is. 9:18, 65:5.

315 The following verses deal with the massive destruction, that is, the destruction of the cities of Sodom (Gen. 19:28), Hai (Josh. 8: 20, 21), Gibea (Jud. 20:38, 40), smoke from leviathan (Job 41:20), etc. In the other portions also, the symbol of destruction is presented. These include, Ps. 18: 8, 68:2, 102:3, 119: 83, Prov. 10:26, Is. 14:31, 34:10, 51.6, Hos. 13:3, Nah. 2.13, Rev. 9:2, 3, 18, 18:9, 18, 19:3.

316 Rev. 14:11.

317 2 Sam. 22:9, Ps. 74:1.

318 The J narrative Gen. 19:28 is noted for God's mercy to Lot. Eugene H. Maly, "Genesis," *The Jerome Bible Commentary,* edited by Raymond Brown, S.S. (London: Geoffrey Chapman, 1968), 21.

theophany.[319] It was coming like the smoke from a kiln or furnace.[320] The purpose of smoke is to obscure man's vision and is presented in the Bible as a symbol of pollution.[321] God destroyed the cities of Sodom, Ai and Gibea with fire since they became unholy. Purity is the requirement of theophany. In the burnt offerings the smoke went skywards and it was described as an 'aroma' pleasing to the Lord (Lev. 1:14). The animal carcasses left behind after the sacrifices were also burnt.[322] Though fire can purify, it produces smoke which is dangerous to human beings. At that time the threat of carbon monoxide created by smoke was unknown. Smoke, pollutes the atmosphere on burning tonnes of waste, destroys the pristine beauty of the universe and contributes to global warming. The modern capitalist industrial society together with its consumerist 'brood of vipers' (Mtt. 3:7), make the earth a hell of burning fire.

5.4.3 *Hell as Burning Fire*

Hades/Hell (Rev. 6:8) is pictured as a place of ungodliness and destruction, and plague, pestilence, famine and droughts are associated with it.[323] Hell is of two types; *Hades* and *Gahanna*. *Hades* is the interim place of the soul after death from which it is delivered at the resurrection (Rev. 20:14).[324] *Gahanna* is a permanent place where the person will be tormented permanently after resurrection (Mk. 9:43, 48). In the Old Testament, the Valley of Hinnom (Jer.

---

319 Ex. 19:18, Son. 3:6, Is. 4:2, 6:4, Rev. 8:4, 15:8.

320 Gordon J. Wenham, *Word Biblical Commentary*, edited by David A. Hubbard and Glenn W. Barker, vol. 2 (Texas: Word Books Publisher, 1987), 59.

321 John I. Durham, *Word Biblical Commentary*, edited by David A. Hubbard and Glenn W. Barker, vol. 3 (Texas: Word Books Publisher, 1987), 271.

322 D. G. Reid, "Sacrifice and Temple Service," *Dictionary of New Testament Practices*, edited by Craig A. Evans and Stanley E. Porter (Leicester: InterVarsity Press, 2000), 1040.

323 David E. Aune, *Word Biblical Commentary,* vol. 52B (Nashville: Thomas Nelson Publishers, 1998), 403.

324 Joachim Jeremias, "Hades," *Theological Dictionary of the New Testament,* edited by Gerhard Kittel (Grand Rapids, MI: William B. Eerdmans Publishing Company, 1964), 148.

7:32, 19:6, Is. 31:9, 66:24) could be equated with the hell of the last judgment. The bad reputation of this place has come from the practice of sacrifices offered to Moloch during the reign of Ahaz and Manasseh (2 Kin. 16:3, 21:6).[325] Hence, this name is to be equated with the eschatological fire of hell. Those who fall victim to the judgment shall be subjected to everlasting fire (Mtt. 5:22, 23:33). At present also the unquenched fire is a common sight in this valley. It is because of impurities that waste is put into fire. Though fire can purify, it is at the cost of the environment. The practice of burning even toxic waste or municipal rejects can make the earth a *Gahanna* of everlasting fire, making a threat to life. Heaven or hell is not to be understood as metaphysical realities, but as places on earth where life is abundant or destructive. *Gahanna* leads to a state of suffering and thus to destruction where life is difficult as we are alienated from God. Burning comes as a result of waste situation which distorts the face and beauty of the earth. Its grandeur can be restored if there is no burning of waste; this can be achieved through reduction of or zero waste culture so as to keep us endeared to God.

5.5 Dumping/Land Filling of Waste in the Kidron Valley

Dumping of waste was done for land filling in Israel as a means to dispose of waste, especially in the Kidron Valley. Geographically, Kidron valley is a dumping yard which lies in between the Mount of Olives and Jerusalem. The place was used to destroy pagan artefacts (1Kin. 15:13).[326] It was during the reign of Asa (ca. 910- 896) who destroyed the Ashera Pole, which his mother Maacah had made in the valley.[327] It is also associated with the destruction of the pagan shrines during the period of Hezekiah (2 Chr. 29:16, 30:14) and

325 Joachim Jeremias, "Gehenna," *Theological Dictionary of the New Testament,* edited by Gerhard Kittel (Grand Rapids, MI: William B. Eerdmans Publishing Company, 1964), 657-658.

326 Derek Williams, *New Concise Bible Dictionary* (Leicester: InterVarsity Press, 1989), 300.

327 Paul R. House, *The American Commentary,* vol. 8 (Taylor University: Broadman and Holman Publishers, 1995), 196-197.

Josiah (2 Kin. 23:4-6). The place is also the location of a number of ancient tombs, which lie at the eastern side. This place was selected because of its proximity to the city walls and convenience to the Temple.[328] The valley was used as a dumping site, and through dumping the process of landfill also had taken place. At present, this place is used to dump garbage and burn trash. These entire mean that waste, either in the form of artefacts or corpses, was disposed of outside the city boundary so that it would not make any hindrance to the public. The only difference between the OT Kidron Valley and the modern Kidron valleys is that, the first one was selected so as not to disturb the comfortable living of people, whereas the second ones, though far from the cities, nonetheless continue to disturb the rural people.

5.6 Waste as Resource: Alternative Use of Waste

Waste can be used in different ways; one person's waste can be anothers' resource. And waste management is a relative term, that is, the concept of waste management differs from person to person and from context to context. Waste can be used as fuel pellets and also for firewood. The use of dried cow dung as fuel was a common sight in Indian villages. This could be seen as an alternative use of waste. A similar episode is mentioned in Ezek. 39: 9 and 10 where all kinds of weapons made of wood were used as fire wood for seven years. There was no need to cut down trees for firewood.[329] This practice has an

328 The place is also known as the "King's Garden" (Neh. 3:15) or "King's Valley" (2 Sam. 18:18), because Absalom had built his monument there. The famous tombs include the tombs of Absolom, Jehoshaphat, Bene Hezir and Zechariah. Joel F. Drinkard, "Kidron," *Harper Collins Bible Dictionary*, edited by Paul J. Achtemeier (Bangalore: Theological Publications in India, 2009), 566-567. The valley is famous for a brook. Its first mention was in the Bible as a place which David crossed (2 Kings. 20:20) and only once is mentioned in the NT (Jn. 18:1). The place is identified as the valley of Jehoshaphat. John L. Gillman, "Kidron," *Eerdmans Dictionary of the Bible*, edited by David Noel Freedman (Grand Rapids, MI: William B. Eerdmans Publishing Company, 2000), 765-766.

329 This passage is used to give hope to the people of Judah during the Babylonian exile under the rule of Nebuchadnezzar. Charles H. Dyer, "Ezekiel," *The Bible*

environmental function also. Instead of burning the whole weapons *en masse* they were used as fire wood. This could serve two functions; one is the systematic management of the accumulation of waste and the other is to meet their daily needs by using them as firewood. Here there is a controlled release of smoke so that the environment can easily absorb it. It becomes anti-environment when smoke is released beyond the nature's capacity to absorb it.

5.7 The Waste Concept in Relation to Judas and Jesus

The waste concepts of Judas and Jesus represent the relational aspect of waste management. Judas was critical about the wastage of labour, money and resources even though it was done for a religious purpose; at the same time Jesus was going one step further and resisting the throw-away culture, was revealed in the following two incidents.

5.7.1 *Judas and the Concept of Waste*

(Mtt. 26:6-13, Mk. 14:3-11, Lk. 7:36-50, Jn. 12:1-8)
These verses describe a woman, variously identified as Mary the sister of Lazarus, or possibly Mary Magdalene, anointing Jesus either at the house of Simon the leper (Mtt., Mk. Lk.) or at the house of Lazarus (Jn.) in Bethany; objections were raised at the waste of the costly ointment, which was worth more than three hundred *denarii*.[330] During dinner it was customary that the host should wash the feet of the guest, who in turn was reluctant for this to be done. It was in this context that the woman anointed Jesus.

The Synoptics as well as the Johannine gospel provides different versions about who made the comment on wasting; the 'disciples' (Mtt. 26:8), 'some' (Mk. 14:4) and Judas, the Iscariot (Jn. 12:4). Luke only reserves his comment. Matthew was more concerned about the price of the alabaster/perfume; in Matthew the complaint

---

Knowledge Commentary: Old Testament, edited by John F. Walvoord and Roy B. Zuck (Hyderabad: Authentic, 2010), 1302.

330 A dinarii was a normal day's earning in Palestine (Mtt. 20:2) and three hundred dinarii was a year's earning. James R. Edwards, *The Gospel According to Mark* (Grand Rapids, MI: William B. Eerdmans Publishing Company, 2002), 413.

was a silent murmuring.[331] To justify 'the evil intention' of Judas, he was referred to as the treasurer of the Twelve, and a thief (Jn. 12:6). In Matthew and Mark, the succeeding verses describe Judas accepting (the promise of) money (Mtt. 26:15, Mk. 14:11) from the Sanhedrin for the betrayal of Jesus. The form criticism of 'why this waste?' can lead us to take literally what is said, though it might have been a commentary on the incident by the early Christian community.[332]

The views of the disciples/some/Judas represented the popular concept of wastage. Despite his economy, Judas was called a traitor by the Gospel writers, and even his concern over this extravagant act was interpreted as his greedy nature.[333] Judas was a member of the Zealots, a radical Galilee resistance movement against Roman imperialism. In spite of their strict organizational structure and discipline, the Zealots used to loot the houses of the wealthy, murdering the owners and setting ablaze the houses of the supporters of Rome.[334] Hence they were identified as thieves and as a Zealot Judas became a victim of such a coinage by John. The Zealots' economy was against the colonial economy of the Roman imperialism. This colonial society wanted the accumulation of resources which led to abundance and finally to wastage; on the other hand the Zealots wanted equal distribution by managing waste. To Judas the production and the consumption of the perfume involved the exploitation of the poor, their labour and the savings of the marginalized community as well. He was countering such an attitude by showing his concern for the poor. As treasurer of the Twelve, he was mediating between Jesus and

331 Robert H. Gundry, *Matthew: A Commentary on His Literary and Theological Art* (Grand Rapids, MI: William B. Eerdmans Publishing Company, 1982), 520.

332 Sherman B. Johnson and George A. Buttrick, "The Gospel According to St. Matthew," *The Interpreter's Bible* (Nashville: Abington Press, 1951), 569.

333 Israel Selvanayagam, "Apostle Judas! You Have a Special Appeal on Dialogue on Power and Authority," *Arasaradi Journal of Theological Reflection* 20 (July-December, 2007): 58.

334 Solomon Victus, "Jesus Approach to Proto- Zionism (The Zealot Movement)," *Arasaradi Journal of Theology* 23/ 1 & 2 (January-December, 2010): 1-3.

the poor, as can be construed from Jn. 13: 29. This is not possible without concern for the poor.

5.7.2 *Jesus and the Concept of Waste*

The waste concept of Judas differs from that of the woman and Jesus as well. Paul Tillich calls the anointing a 'holy waste,' which comes from the abundance of the woman's heart. The woman represents the ecstatic element in relation to God whereas Judas/the disciples represent the reasonable element.[335] Though Jesus was countering the stand of Judas, he himself had his own idea of the poor, wastage and so on which can be seen in the feeding of the multitude. In Mark the question came as a result of an early clash between the market mind and the life of the spirit. Jesus was condemning such a middle class attitude which measured everything in terms of the current market economy.[336] There are criticisms of Judas also. He was neither a victim of circumstances nor a pawn in the hands of the Sanhedrin, but he himself had chosen his destiny.[337] The needs of the poor should not be measured in economic terms only and true care for the poor is focused on when they identify Jesus (Mtt. 25:40) with the poor.[338] It becomes waste when something loses its relevance and becomes useless. To Jesus neither the ointment nor the anointment was waste. The woman was doing the act of anointing ahead of Jesus' burial. From Judas to Jesus the relational aspect of waste becomes transparent. That is 'waste' is not absolute.

---

335 Paul Tillich, *The New Being* (New York: Charles Scribner's Sons, 1955), 46-47.

336 Frederick C. Grant and Halford E. Luccock, "The Gospel According to St. Mark," *The Interpreter's Bible* (Nashville: Abington Press, 1951), 868-869.

337 James R. Edwards, *The Gospel According to Mark* (Grand Rapids, MI: William B. Eerdmans Publishing Company), 418.

338 Michael Fallon MSC, *The Gospel According to Saint Mark* (Bangalore: Asian Trading Corporation, 2002), 238.

5.7.2.1 Waste Management as Resistance to the Throw-away Culture

(Mtt. 14:21, Mk. 6:43, Lk. 9:17 and Jn. 6:12)

All these verses say that the disciples collected 12 baskets full of fragments after feeding the five thousand. Mtt., Lk., and Jn. (Mtt. 14:21, Lk. 9:17, Jn. 6:12) speak of the broken pieces or fragments. Mark includes the fish also (6:43). Jn. 6:12 only records Jesus' comments to the disciples 'to gather the fragments left over so that nothing may be lost.' It is sinful to have wastefulness and having abundance is reason for waste. It was the pieces or fragments, not crumbs or scraps, which the disciples collected at the encouragement of Jesus.[339] Through that Jesus was countering the throwaway consumerist culture, a form of resistance. In the Temple cleansing incident also, Jesus was resisting the urbanized culture which exploits the poor, takes away their rights. Jesus did not want to make the hill area a dumping ground with the surplus of resources which later becomes waste. He respected the local surrounding and knew well the worth of that place. He was honouring two things; the right of the earth to be pollution free and the right of the community to be sufficiently fed. Jesus was encouraging the disciples to collect the fragments which can be used as food for the poor. This pericope reveals how effectively waste management can be done by being ecofriendly and pro-poor. This also opens the depth of Jesus' zero-waste economy.

5.7.2.2 Waste Management through Community Participation

Waste management is not an effort to be done compartmentally, but needs to be done holistically. For community participation, strengthening the civil society is a must. Jesus incorporated the disciples'/ community participation for the management of waste. Collecting the broken pieces after a banquet was a Jewish custom. The Jews carried little food baskets so that they can have food as per

339 William Hendriksen, *The Gospel of John* (London: The Banner of Truth Trust, 1954), 223.

the Jewish food laws.[340] Therefore, the twelve baskets belonged to the twelve disciples which correspond to the twelve tribes of Israel.[341] Though it was not mentioned, Jesus also took part in the collection of the fragments. It is also the symbol of totality and fruitfulness of the task. We are not sure what they did with the rest. There is no reason to disbelieve that they did not throw away the leftovers. Either they might have kept the fragments for later consumption or used them as pig feed, because at that time pig rearing was very popular. Waste management is not effective without community participation. Here who will take the initiative is a matter of dispute. Without waiting for the other, each individual has to voluntarily take the initiative for waste management.

5.8 Towards a Zero Waste Theology

From all these and similar concepts and instances, the theology that arises is the Zero Waste Theology (ZWT), which the researcher wants to propose as part of eco-theology. ZWT emphasizes the need to respect the environment's right to be pollution free, to keep our surroundings *tob* and make *kadhosh,* making the harmful harmless and returning to nature. God has created the world as good, and human beings have no right to make it bad which the accumulation of waste creates. Any form of human intervention to nature should be to create a zero waste economy. Though the concept of waste is relational, human participation should be to make a zero waste society thus making life affirming and useful, not life denying and useless.

340 Sherman B. Johnson and George A. Buttrick, "The Gospel According to St. Matthew," *The Interpreter's Bible* (Nashville: Abington Press, 1951), 431.

341 Benedict T. Viviano, O.P., "The Gospel According to Matthew," *The Jerome Bible Commentary*, edited by Raymond E. Brown, Joseph A. Fitzmyer, S. J. and Roland E. Murphy, O. Carm (Bangalore: Theological Publication in India, 1990), 659.

Conclusion

Waste is the leviathan of the modern industrial system.[342] Like the restoration of the biological cycle, there should be a restoration of the material cycle so as to restore the value, the energy and the work contained in the thrown away material.[343] Developing a theology of waste can lead us to understand the real value of the material thrown out. Even though the concepts of waste and waste management are relative, we have to understand the significance of the concepts. God has created everything as good and holy with a divine purpose. It is sinful to interfere with the divine purpose by human action; if any part of creation is distorted through waste dumping, a human action, it is time to restore it to the original cycle. Methods of waste management vary, whether burying, burying or dumping. These arc also relative. Someone's waste can be another's resource. Waste management should not be done without regard to others' feelings and surroundings. For that the role of taking initiatives and strengthening civil society, individual and community participation are integral.

342 Robin Murray, "Zero Waste," *Frontier* 42/14 (October 18-24, 2009): 14.

343 Ibid., 15.

General Conclusion

Waste is a reality created by every one of us and has to be dealt with in our day to day life. It is the outcome of human and domestic animal activities. Its generation started from the very moment of the Creation of living beings on earth and passed through different ages and civilizations, aggravated by urbanization. From time immemorial human society has been struggling to dispose of waste which ultimately resulted in its being dumped in uninhabited places, roadsides, water sources and even in villages where people were unaware of its dangers. Waste accumulation did not evade any nation whether developed, developing or underdeveloped in nature. India is also in the grip of a waste crisis, and its management has a centuries' long history dating back to the creation of the caste structure on the basis of people's occupation. Though the concept of consumerism is a recent phenomenon, its inspiration came from the colonial structure and the growth of industrialism, which gradually conquered Indian cities with foreign products, continued and aggravated by the neoliberal policies after the 1990s. Urban people are responding to the refuse of consumerism by throwing their waste into villages and making them into dumping yards despite local people's resistance. The Local Self Governing Bodies which have been entrusted with the responsibility of waste management had taken up the issue and attempted to sort it out through various means including the construction of waste treatment plants inside or outside their administrative territories depending on their attitude, availability of space, technical support, and the response of the people with or without success. The management of waste becomes a problem if there is even a deviation in any of these. Thiruvananthapuram, Kerala's capital city, also wanted to tackle the garbage crisis at the initiative of the Corporation through a garbage treatment plant in Vilappilsala, a project started without people's consensus, against which the people resisted through a People's Movement called the Vilappilsala Janakeeya Samithy (VJS).

The anti-garbage treatment plant struggle led by the VJS is the culmination of the decade long Vilappil people's discontent over an ill-managed garbage treatment plant which has been threatening the very existence of the people. Various smaller protest initiatives came from the people and even the religious organizations and leaders such as Bishop Samuel Amritam also tried to handle the issue at the preliminary stage, but this fervour could not be maintained by the succeeding leaderships. The Corporation and the State Government led by opposing political parties tried to harvest the issue, mislead the judiciary, protect their own political interests, play electoral games and hijack the struggle, against which the VJS cautioned the people through grassroots units. The local Panchayat, though it did not support the struggle at the initial stage, was forced to express its solidarity. However, the people's resistance was rewarded with the State Government Order closing the malfunctioning plant, although the legal battle is still going on in the Green Tribunal.

In the arbitrary establishment of the waste treatment plant the Corporation was unmindful of the historical legacy of village's agrarian economy. Even the choice of the place was also unsuitable for the plant as it is near a low lying water body which the villagers were using. The different companies such as the Poabson, the Excel, the Centre for Environment and Development, with whom the Corporation entrusted the responsibility of the management of the plant failed to effectively control pollution, or find a market for the compost, and this ultimately led to making Vilappilsala as a dumping yard. It is against this improper management and polluting atmosphere that the people of the village resisted. The nature of the people's resistance brings about certain remarkable factors as how to lead the struggle from a local level. Even though some of their resistance methods were common to similar struggles such as demonstrations, shouting slogans, *hartaals*, hunger strikes, road blocks and night vigils, they developed their own resistance methods like delaying the police arrest through deploying women and children in front, preparing *pongala* on the road, the slow drinking of gruel and tying themselves with *saris* and *shawls*. The antagonistic attitude of the Corporation to the struggle was revealed in their complaints to the police who arrested the leaders of the struggle on false charges. However the people showed their strength by taking contributions from the villagers and well-wishers at the initiative of the VJS for finding the bail amount required to release the leaders. As all the villagers were behind the VJS, the local Panchayat felt inferior to the people's movement and they felt challenged by the popular mobilization that VJS was bringing, and this led to the formation of another people's movement under the leadership of the Panchayat called the Samyuktha Samara Samithy (SSS).

The problem that the garbage treatment plant created in Vilappilsala was immeasurable. The people's social life was disrupted because of the plant. They felt unable to live in the village because of so many problems; the stench; water pollution; health problems, for instance breathing difficulties, skin disease, itching, diarrhoea, repeated abortions; mosquitoes, swarms of big flies; stray dogs; rodents; smoke from repeated burning of plastic; and the failure of marriage proposals all these had made their village unfit to live in. Economically the people slowly started selling off their properties which the land mafia took advantage of in a five kilometre radius. In the collective life the State Government and the Corporation tried to extinguish the spirit of the people's struggle using its coercive forces and the Courts. The media tried to cash in the issue, but the local churches, the movements leading similar struggles and environmental activists such as Sarah Joseph, Sugathakumari and sculptor Kanayi Kunjiraman extended their support to the struggle. In fact they were countering the Corporation's motto to produce a 'clean city' at the cost of destroying a rural area, especially Vilappilsala. However, the people felt a sigh of relief after the closure of the plant.

The resistance of the people was against the city dwellers' strong adherence to a throw-away consumerist culture created by the industrial revolution, promoted by neoliberal policies, and propagated and justified through the media. The struggle could unite and mobilize people of the village irrespective of all distinctions and invite supporters from various walks of life and similar organizations under the leadership of the VJS. In spite of all these struggles, the people have their own understanding of waste. They all believe that a wasteless society can never be created. Yet they are practising their own systems of disposal of waste and they are going to the extent of burning plastic which results in the generation of carcinogenic gases. They fought the struggle as a survival issue, not as an environmental problem. Even the members of the people's movement were also the victims of consumerism. Their stand was a double standard. They wanted all consumer benefits and were reluctant to become models for others in waste management and sacrifice their middle class comforts. Even so they remain firm in their opinion, and thus they are determined to disallow the Corporation waste dumping in their backyard, and the willingness to fight another battle if the factory reopens.

The struggle of Vilappilsala raises serious questions about how to address the issues of waste generation, collection, transportation and disposal. It can be done through the involvement of smaller communities whereas waste management is difficult in larger societies. This forces us to think of whether we should reject consumerism, but complete rejection of consumerism is not possible as M. M. Thomas observes. This challenges us to think of a minimalistic living and change of our life style, and the use of alternatives to plastic such as the use of biodegradable plastic in the process of chemichalisation and the inevitability of handling toxic materials; only enlightened communities can implement such solutions. The solution to waste accumulation is not exclusive, it is eclectic, i.e., multidimensional; the use of integrated waste management, that is, the use of 'four R's and one L,'to 'reduce, reuse, recycle, recover and landfill' the residue. Each method is mutually enriching. As part of the source level disposal of waste, composting all the organic waste is the best option which is used to recover energy from waste. Waste management becomes holistic when we practise it from – the micro to the macro level, and for that the community participation is vital. All these could create a zero waste economy.

Regarding the theology of waste and its management, one need to remember that God has created everything as good, that is useful (*tob*) and holy (*kadhosh*) and that it is human action that makes it ugly and unholy. The human responsibility of stewardship is to turn the bad and unholy into good and holy so that it may return to nature for assimilation. The Israelite practice of covering the night soil with soil (Deut. 23:12-14), the first and the second burial system of the dead (2 Kin. 22:20), the burning of the carcasses after sacrifices (Lev. 4:12), the dumping of artefacts in the Kidron Valley (1 Kin. 15:13), the alternative use of waste as fuel pellets (Ezek. 39:9, 10), the creation of smoke and hell as burning fire in the valley of Hinnom (Jer. 7:32), Judas' concern over the wastage of alabaster in Jesus' anointing scene in the four gospels, Jesus' resistance to the throw-away culture by encouraging the disciples to collect the fragments after feeding the five thousand all reveal the depth of waste management and could all be taken up so as to create a theology of waste management called the Zero Waste Theology.

The road to a zero waste economy is sacrificial. 'Zero' doesn't mean 'nothing'; instead it means the maximum or the optimal reduction in the volume of waste through various individual, communities or administrative levels of using available and ecologically sustainable technology. Community participation and strengthening civil society are essential for effective waste management. Waste accumulation comes as result of the NIMBY syndrome of people and there should be a shift in our attitude towards seeing, 'my waste, my property and my responsibility' for the creation of a zero waste economy.

Bibliography

A. Primary Sources

1. Correspondences

Amritam, Samuel. Bishop of the CSI South Kerala Diocese. Letter to the District Collector of Thiruvananthapuram, 16 June 1995.

Burhan. President of the VJS. Letter to the Chief Minister of Kerala, 19 January 2011.

2. Diaries

Johnson, J.C. "Diary Writings." Vilappilsala.

3. Electronic Sources

Vilappilsala Janakeeya Samithy (2012). CD- ROM.

Vilappilsala Struggle. Samyuktha Samara Samithy (16 October 2012). Photographs.

4. Government Documents

Development of Trivandrum Municipality and Corporation. Thiruvananthapuram: Thiruvananthapuram Nagarasabha, 1998.

Vilappil Grama Panchayat Vikasana Report, Janakeeya Asoothranam. Vol. 5. Thiruvananthapuram: Kerala State Planning Board, 1997.

5. Legal Documents

Comments on Report of the Advocate Commission in WP (C) No. 9/2/2012.

Comments on Report of the Environmental Engineer, KSPCB in WP(C) No. 9/2/2012. 23 January 2012.

Gnanadas. *Affidavit Before the Hon'ble High Court of Kerala at Ernakulam, I. A. No. of 2012 in WP (C) No. 9 of 2012.* 2 September 2012.

Manjula Chellur, Ag. CJ., & A. M. Shaffique, J. *Kerala High Court Order I. A. No. 98610 of 2012 in W.P. (C) No. 9 of 2012 (A).* 26 July 2012.

Official Note No. 2180 of Thiruvanathapuram Corporation. 8 March 2012.

P. K. Manoj Kumar and Hena Bahuleyan. *Statement of Facts, Memorandum of Writ Petition Filed under Article 226 of the Constitution of India.* 1 January 2012.

Report on Vilappilsala Biowaste Processing Factory, PCB/TVM- DO/ CO/GEA/09. 18 March 2011.

Report Submitted Before the Hon'ble Advocate Commission of the High Court of Kerala in WP (C) 9/2012 (A) & the Environmental Engineer of the Kerala State Pollution Control Board.

Response to Counter Affidavit Filed by Respondents 6-9 in *WP (C) No. 9 of 2012 (A).*

Submitted before the Environmental Engineer of the KSPCB in *WP (C) 9/2012 (A), the Corporation Secretary.* 8 April 2012.

Submitted before the Hon' ble Advocate Commission of the High Court of Kerala in WP (C) 9/2012 (A) & the Environmental Engineer of the KSPCB, the Corporation Secretary. 14 January 2012.

Susheelkumar. *Enquiry Report against the Complaint Submitted by Nadar Co-Ordination Council against Vilappilsala Waste Factory, No. E1/29/11/CHCV, V.* 18 January 2011.

6. Interviews

Asha. Former Worker of the Garbage Treatment Plant. Interview. 22 September 2013.

Burhan. President of Vilappilsala Janakeeya Samithy. Interview. 4 May 2012.

____________ . Interview. 7 February 2016.

Das. Former Worker of the Garbage Treatment Plant. Interview. 22 Spetember 2013.

Japagjanam. Former Presbyter of CSI Kadampanad. Interview. 28 July 2013.

Johnson. A Resident of Vilappilsala. Interview. 20 April 2013.

Joshy. A Resident of Vilappilsala and the Son of J. C. Johnson. Interview. 25 July 2013.

Kaldharan. Former Worker of the Garbage Treatment Plant. Interview. 11 August 2013

Patel, H. Almitra. Member of Supreme Court Drafting Committee for Solid Waste Management of Class I Cities in India. Interview. 27 October 2012.

Santhosh. JAT of Thiruvananthapuram Corporation. Interview. 13 December 2013.

Sathy Kulumala. Volunteer of VJS. Interview. 9 September 2012.

Sheela. Former Worker of the Garbage Treatment Plant. Interview. 18 April 2013.

Shiva Kailas. Convenor of Samyuktha Samara Samithy. Interview. 24 April 2013.

Vinod. Office Staff in Charge of Solid Waste Management of Thiruvananthapuram Corporation. Interview. 13 December 2013.

7. Newspaper Reports

Desabhimani (Thiruvananthapuram), 22 December 2010.

Janmabhumi (Thiruvananthapuram), 14 February 2012.

Kerala Kaumudi (Thiruvananthapuram), 3 January 2012.

Kerala Kaumudi (Thiruvananthapuram), 7 January 2012.
Kerala Kaumudi (Thiruvananthapuram), 10 January 2012.
Kerala Kaumudi (Thiruvananthapuram), 14 February 2012.
Kerala Kaumudi (Thiruvananthapuram), 12 June 2012.
Kerala Kaumudi (Thiruvananthapuram), 13 June 2012.
Kerala Kaumudi (Thiruvananthapuram), 18 June 2012.
Kerala Kaumudi (Thiruvananthapuram), 21 June 2012.
Kerala Kaumudi (Thiruvananthapuram), 27 June 2012.
Kerala Kaumudi (Thiruvananthapuram), 1 August 2012.
Kerala Kaumudi (Thiruvananthapuram), 4 August 2012.
Madhyamam (Thiruvananthapuram), 14 February 2012.
Malayala Manorama (Thiruvananthapuram), 2 December 1995.
Malayala Manorama (Thiruvananthapuram), 5 October 1996.
Malayala Manorama (Thiruvananthapuram), 25 July 2010.
Malayala Manorama (Thiruvananthapuram), 8 February 2012.
Malayala Manorama (Thiruvananthapuram), 5 April 2012.
Malayala Manorama (Thiruvananthapuram), 12 April 2012.
Malayala Manorama (Thiruvananthapuram), l2 June 2012.
Malayala Manorama (Thiruvananthapuram), 25 July 2012.
Malayala Manorama (Thiruvananthapuram), 1 August 2012.
Malayala Manorama (Thiruvananthapuram), 4 August 2012.
Malayala Manorama (Thiruvananthapuram), 15 August 2012.
Malayala Manorama (Thiruvananthapuram), l1 September 2012.
Malayala Manorama (Thiruvananthapuram), 7 September 2012.
Malayala Manorama (Thiruvananthapuram), 14 October 2012.
Malayala Manorama (Thiruvananthapuram), 18 October 2012.
Malayala Manorama (Thiruvananthapuram), 12 December 2012.
Malayala Manorama (Thiruvananthapuram), 5 June 2013.
Malayala Manorama (Thiruvananthapuram), 5 June 2013.
Malayala Manorama (Thiruvananthapuram), 2 July 2013.
Malayala Manorama (Thiruvananthapuram), 28 February 2016.
Mangalam (Thiruvananthapuram), 14 February 2012.

Mathrubhumi (Thiruvananthapuram), 5 October 1996.

Mathrubhumi (Thiruvananthapuram), 9 February 2011.

Mathrubhumi (Thiruvananthapuram), 13 February 2011.

Mathrubhumi (Thiruvananthapuram), 15 April 2011.

Mathrubhumi (Thiruvananthapuram), 4 May 2011.

Mathrubhumi (Thiruvananthapuram), 29 July 2011.

Mathrubhumi (Thiruvananthapuram), 2 August 2011.

Mathrubhumi (Thiruvananthapuram), 20 September 2011.

Mathrubhumi (Thiruvananthapuram), 14 February 2012.

Mathrubhumi (Thiruvananthapuram), 24 May 2012.

Mathrubhumi Nattuvarthamanam (Thiruvananthapuram), 22 December 2010.

Mathrubhumi Nattuvarthamanam (Thiruvananthapuram), 30 January 2011.

Mathrubhumi Nattuvarthamanam (Thiruvanathapuram), 19 April 2011.

Mathrubhumi Nattuvarthamanam (Thiruvananthapuram), 1 May 2011.

Mathrubhumi Nattuvarthamanam (Thiruvananthapuram), 21 September 2011.

Metro Manorama (Thiruvananthapuram), 27 July 2012.

Metro Manorama (Thiruvananthapuram), 4 August 2012.

The Hindu (Madurai), 12 August 2012.

The Hindu (Thiruvananthapuram), 29 August 2011.

The Hindu (Thiruvananthapuram), 20 September 2011.

The Hindu (Thiruvananthapuram), 14 February 2012.

The Hindu (Thiruvananthapuram), 2 October 2012.

The Hindu (Thiruvananthapuram), 11 October 2012.

The Hindu (Thiruvananthapuram), 12 October 2012.

The Hindu (Thiruvananthapuram), 15 October 2012.

The Hindu (Thiruvananthapuram), 16 October 2012.

The Hindu (Thiruvananthapuram), 15 November 2012.

The Hindu (Thiruvananthapuram), 8 January 2013.

The Hindu (Thiruvananthapuram), 24 January 2013.

The Hindu (Thiruvananthapuram), 25 January 2013.

The Hindu (Thiruvananthapuram), 1 February 2013.

The Hindu (Thiruvananthapuram), 12 March 2013.

The Hindu (Thiruvananthapuram), 28 February 2016.

Veekshanam (Thiruvananthapuram), 14 February 2012.

8. Pamphlets and Newsletters

"July 24 Karidinamayi Acharikkunnu." VJS Pamphlet, Vilappilsala, 20 July 2011.

"Vijayawada Njangal Marannittilla." VJS Pamphlet, Vilappilsala, 5 April 2013.

"Vaidyudi Utpadanam Chavaril Ninum." Corporation Pamphlet, Thiruvananthapuram, 2000.

Ram, L Hari. VJS News Letter. Vilappilsala, 2012.

B. Secondary Sources

1. Books

Agarwal, S. K. *Air Pollution*. New Delhi: A.P.H. Publishing Corporation, 2005.

Bhatia, S. C. *Wealth from Waste*. Vol. 1. New Delhi: Atlantic Publishers and Distributors Pvt. Ltd., 2007.

_________. *Solid and Hazardous Waste Management*. New Delhi: Atlantic Publishers and Distributors (P) Ltd., 2007.

_________. *Wealth from Waste: Agricultural, Food and Chemical Processing Waste*. Vol. 1. New Delhi: Atlantic Publishers and Distributors (P) Ltd., 2007.

Brown, Raymond. *The Message of Deuteronomy*. Leicester: InterVarsity Press, 1993.

Chandran, M. Vjaya, et al., "Remote Sensing Applications in Identifying Suitabale Sites for Solid Waste Disposal in Visakhapatanam, Andhra Pradesh, India." In *Environmental*

Engineering. Edited by Arvind Kumar and Shishir Suman Mishra. Delhi: Daya Publishing House, 2010.

Craigie, Peter C. *The Book of Deuteronomy*. Grand Rapids, MI: William B. Eerdmans Publishing Company, 1976.

Deb, Debal. *Beyond Developementality: Constrcuting Inclusive Freedom and Sustainabaility*. Delhi: Daanish Books, 2009.

Desroches, John. *The India We Want to Build*. Vol. 2. Bangalore: Centre for Social Action, 1995.

Dhameja, Suresh, K. *Environment Engineering and Management*. New Delhi: S. K. Kataria and Sons, 2002.

Edwards, James R. *The Gospel According to Mark*. Grand Rapids, MI: William B. Eerdmans Publishing Company, 2002.

Evans, Gareth. *Biowaste and Biologial Waste Treatment*. London: James and James, 2005.

Guha, Ramachandra. *Environmentalaism: A Global History*. New Delhi: Oxford University Press, 2000.

Hay, Peter. *A Companion to Environmental Thought*. Edinburgh: Edinburgh University Press, 2002.

Higgins, Roger J. "Environmental Management of New Mining Option." In *Enviromental Management of Solid Waste: Dredged Materials and Mine Tailings*. Edited by W. Salomons and U. Forstner. Verlag: Springer, 1988.

Jagadeesan, Hema. "Pollution." In *Understanding Environment*. Edited by Kiran B. Chhokar, Mamta Pandya and Meena Raghunathan. New Delhi: Sage Publications, 2005.

Jha, D. K. *Environmental Studies*. Kanpur: Bhaskar Publications, 2012.

John, V. J. *The Ecological Vision of Jesus: Nature in the Parables of Mark*. Thiruvalla and Bangalore: CSS & BTTBPSA, 2002.

Kumarappa, Bharathan. *Capitalism, Socialism or Villagism?* Rajghat: Sarva Seva Sangh Prakashan, 1965.

Misra, P. N. *Environment Pollution and Its Control*. New Delhi: Sumit Enterprises, 2007.

Mitra, Abhijit. *Foundation of Environmental Science*. Delhi: Narendra Publishing House, 2000.

Mohd, Salahuddin. *Waste Management in Urban Area*. Delhi: B.R. Publishing Corporation, 2011.

Moore, Ruth. *Man in the Environment*. New Delhi: TATA McGraw Hill Publishing Company Ltd., 1975.

Nair, K. N. and Sridhar R, eds. *Cleaning Up Kerala. Studies in Self-help in Dealing with Solid Waste*. Delhi: Daanish Books, 2005.

Nathanson, Jerry A. *Basic Environmental Technology, Water Supply, Waste Management and Pollution Control*. New Delhi: PHI Learning Pvt. Ltd., 2009.

Pawar, S.N, R. B. Patil and S. A. Salunkhe, eds. *Environmental Movements in India*. Jaipur: Rawat Publications, 2005.

Prabhakar, V. K., ed. *Solid Waste Management*. New Delhi: Anmol Publications Pvt. Ltd., 2001.

Prasad, P. N. and T. R. Amarnath. *Waste Pollution and Its Control*. New Delhi: Crescent Publishing Corporation, 2010.

Purohit, S. S. *Green Technology: An Approach for Sustainable Development*. Jodhpur: Agrobios India, 2008.

Radhakrishnan, R. *Bio-Medical Waste Management*. New Delhi: Sumit Enterprises, 2006.

Ramachandran, K. and K. Sahadevan. *Malinyasamskaranam Kharamalinyangal: Prasnanagalum Pariharangalum-Oru Padhanam*. Thrissur: Current Books, 2003.

Sareen, Shalini. *Urban Pollution and Its Management*. New Delhi: IVY Publishing House, 2005.

Singh, Randhir. *Contemporary Ecological Crisis: A Marxist View*. Delhi: Aakar Books, 2009.

Sinha, Jayantha, et al., "Vermi Compost: Its Proper and Successful Application in the Cultivation of Aloe *barbadensis*." In *Pollution and Biodiversity: Biosocial Aspect*. Edited by Arvind Kumar. Delhi: Daya Publishing House, 2009.

Sinha, Rajiv K. and Ambuj K. Sinha. *Waste Management*. Jaipur: INA Shree Publications, 2000.

Sirohi, K. S. *Environment Change and Management.* New Delhi: Pearl Books, 2009.

Suresh, Lal B. and Ravinder. M. "Environmental Pollution: Impact on Health and Economy: An Overview Study." In *Global Environmental Issues Empirical Evidences.* Edited by Lal B. Suresh. New Delhi: Serials Publications, 2010.

Tillich, Paul. *The New Being.* New York: Charles Scribner's Sons, 1955.

Tripathi, K. T. *Current Topics in Environment Sciences.* New Delhi: Pearl Books, 2009.

Ujang, Zaini and Morgens Henze, eds. *Municipal Waste Water Management in Developing Countries: Principles and Engineering.* Lyngby: IWA Publishing, 2006.

Vasisth, Kamal. *Environmental Change.* New Delhi: Maxford Books, 2008.

Vesilund, P. Arne, William Worrel and Reinhart. *Solid Waste Engineering.* Bangalore: Bill Stenquist, 2002.

Wenham, Gordon J. *The Book of Leviticus.* Grand Rapids, MI: William B. Eerdmans Publishing Company, 1979.

Wentz, Charles A. *Hazarduous Waste Management.* New York: McGraw- Hill Book Company, 1989.

Wielenga, Bas. *Towards an Eco-Just Society.* Bangalore: Centre for Social Action, 1999.

2. Bible Commentaries

Aune, David E. *Word Biblical Commentary.* Vol. 52B. Nashville: Thomas Nelson Publishers, 1998.

Blenkinsopp, Joseph. "Deuteronomy." *The Jerome Bible Commentary.* Edited by Raymond E. Brown, Joseph A. Fitzmyer, S.J. and Roland E. Murphy, O. Carm. Bangalore: Theological Publication in India, 1990, 94-109.

Cassuto, U. *A Commentary on the Book of Genesis.* Translated from the Hebrew by Israel Abrahams. Jerusalem: The Hebrew University, 1961.

Clifford, Richard J., SJ and Roland E. Murphy, O. Carm. "Genesis." *The Jerome Bible Commentary*. Edited by Raymond E. Brown, Joseph A. Fitzmyer, S. J. and Roland E. Murphy, O. Carm. Bangalore: Theological Publication in India, 1990, 8-43.

Deere, Jack S. "Deuteronomy." *The Bible Knowledge Commentary: Old Testament*. Edited by John F. Walvoord and Roy B. Zuck. Hyderabad: Authentic, 2010, 304-354.

Driver, S. R. *A Critical and Exegetical Commentary on Deuteronomy*. 3rd ed. Edinburgh: T & T Clark, 1996.

Durham, John I. *Word Biblical Commentary*. Edited by David A. Hubbard and Glenn W. Barker. Vol. 3. Texas: Word Books Publisher, 1987.

Dyer, Charles H. "Ezekiel." *The Bible Knowledge Commentary: Old Testament*. Edited by John F. Walvoord and Roy B. Zuck. Hyderabad: Authentic, 2010, 1225-1317.

Edwards, James R. *The Gospel According to Mark*. Grand Rapids, MI: William B. Eerdmans Publishing Company, 2002.

Fritsch, C. T. *Genesis: The Layman's Bible Commentary*. London: Bloomsbury, 1960.

Gaebelein, Frank E., ed. *The Expositor's Bible Commentary*. Vol. 3. Michigan: Zondervan Publishing House, 1992.

Grant, Frederick C. and Halford E. Luccock, "The Gospel According to St. Mark," *The Interpreter's Bible*. Nashville: Abington Press, 1951, 629-917.

Gundry, Robert H. *Matthew: A Commentary on His Literary and Theological Art.* Grand Rapids, MI: William B. Eerdmans Publishing Company, 1982.

Hartley, John E. *Word Bible Commentary*. Vol. 4. Texas: Word Books Publisher, 1992.

Hendriksen, William. *The Gospel of John*. London: The Banner of Truth Trust, 1954.

House, Paul R. *The American Commentary.* Vol. 8. Taylor University: Broadman and Holman Publishers, 1995, 196-197.

Johnson, Sherman B. and George A. Buttrick. "The Gospel According to St. Matthew." *The Interpreter's Bible*. Nashville: Abington Press, 1951, 231-629.

Lindsey, F. Duane. "Deuteronomy." *The Word Bible Commentary: Old Testament.* Edited by John F. Walvoord and Roy B. Zuck. Hyderabad: Authentic, 2010, 163-214.

Maly, Eugene H. "Genesis." The *Jerome Bible Commentary*. Edited by Raymond Brown S. S. London: Geoffrey Chapman, 1968, 7-46.

Merrill, Eugene H. *The New American Commentary.* Vol. 4. Dallas: Broadman and Holman Publishers, 1994.

MSC, Michael Fallon. *The Gospel According to Saint Mark*. Bangalore: Asian Trading Corporation, 2002.

O. P., Benedict T. Viviano. "The Gospel According to Matthew." *The Jerome Bible Commentary*. Edited by Raymond E. Brown, Joseph A. Fitzmyer, S. J. and Roland E. Murphy, O. Carm. Bangalore: Theological Publication in India, 1990, 630-674.

Rooker, Mark F. *The New American Commentary*. Vol. 3A. Nashville: Broadman and Holman Publishers, 2000.

Sailhamer, John H. "Genesis." *The Expositior's Bible Commentary*. Edited by Frank E. Gaebelein. Vol. 2. Michigan: Zondervan Publishing House, 1990, 1-284.

Skinner, John. *A Critical Exegetical Commentary on Genesis*. 2nd ed. Edinburgh: T & T Clark, 1994.

Von Rad, Gerhard. *Genesis: A Commentary.* Translated by John H. Marks. London: SCM Press Ltd., 1961.

Wenham, Gordon J. *Word Biblical Commentary*. Edited by David A. Hubbard and Glenn W. Barker. Vol. 1. Texas: Word Books Publisher, 1987.

Wenham, Gordon J. *Word Biblical Commentary*. Edited by David A. Hubbard and Glenn W. Barker. Vol. 2. Texas: Word Books Publisher, 1987.

3. Bible Dictionaries

Collins, Raymond F. "Good." *The Anchor Bible Dictionary.* Edited by David Noel Freedman. Vol. 2. New York: Doubleday, 1992, 1074-1075.

Drinkard, Joel F. "Kidron." *Harper Collins Bible Dictionary*. Edited by Paul J. Achtemeier. Bangalore: Theological Publications in India, 2009, 566-567.

Gillman, John L. "Kidron." *Eerdmans Dictionary of the Bible.* Edited by David Noel Freedman. Grand Rapids, MI: William B. Eerdmans Publishing Company, 2000, 765-766.

Jeremias, Joachim. "Gehenna." *Theological Dictionary of the New Testament.* Edited by Gerhard Kittel. Grand Rapids, MI: William B. Eerdmans Publishing Company, 1964, 657-658.

Jeremias, Joachim. "Hades." *Theological Dictionary of the New Testament.* Edited by Gerhard Kittel. Grand Rapids, MI: William B. Eerdmans Publishing Company, 1964, 146-149.

McCane, B. R. "Burial Practices, Jewish." *Dictionary of New Testament Practices*. Edited by Craig A. Evans and Stanley E. Porter. Leicester: InterVarsity Press, 2000, 172-175.

Reid, D. G. "Sacrifice and Temple Service." *Dictionary of New Testament Practices.* Edited by Craig A. Evans and Stanley E. Porter. Leicester: InterVarsity Press, 2000, 1036-1050.

Smith, W. T. and W. J. Harrelson. "Holiness." *Dictionary of the Bible.* Edited by James Hastings. Edinburgh: T & T Clark, 1963, 387-388.

Stoebe, H. J. "Good." *Theological Lexicon of the Old Testament.* Translated by Mark E. Biddle. Edited by Ernst Jenni and Claus Westermann. Vol. 2. Massachusetts: Henrickson Publishers, 2004, 486-495.

Williams, Derek. *New Concise Bible Dictionary.* Leicester: InterVarsity Press, 1989, 300.

4. Periodicals

"A Fill of Waste." *Down to Earth* 4/20 (March 15, 1996): 24-26.

"A Study in Chennai City." *Economic and Political Weekly* 41/22 (June 3, 2006): 2259-2267.

"Hospital Waste: Management Morass." *Down to Earth* 5/31 (May 31, 1996): 27-31.

"Not in My Backyard." *Economic and Political Weekly* 47/29 (July 21, 2012): 8.

"Plastic Go Eco-friendly." *Down to Earth* 8/7 (August 31, 1999): 52-53.

"Plastic Surgery." *Down to Earth* 7/9 (September 30, 1998): 5.

"Plastic Unlimited." *Down to Earth* 9/14 (December 15, 2000): 20-23.

"Plastic Unwrapped." *Economic and Pilitical Weekly* 33/52 (December 26, 1998): 32-89.

"Public Waste Private Enterprise." *Gobar Times Down to Earth Supplement* 2/1 (May 31, 2002): 62-69.

"The Burning Question." *Down to Earth* 7/7 (February 15, 1998): 23-24.

"The Flush Toilet is Ecologically Mindless." *Down to Earth* 10/19 (February 28, 2002): 28-38.

"The Morning After." *Down to Earth* 17/16 (January 1-15, 2009): 47.

"We Need to Talk about Toilets." *New Internationalist* 414 (August, 2008): 6-9.

Achuthan, A. and K. Sreedharan. "Keralathil Paristhithinayathinenthu?" *Mathrubhoomi Azhchapathippu* 84/15 (June 11-17, 2006): 29-33.

Agarwal, Ravi. "Packaging Plastic Policy." *Down to Earth* 8/18 (February 15, 2000): 55.

Agarwal, Ravi. "Cleansing Chronicle." *Down to Earth* 9/23 (April 30, 2001): 54-55.

Ahmed, Kazimuddin. "Living in Hell." *Down to Earth* 7/18 (February 15, 1999): 48-49.

Albina, Alice. "In the Pay of Plastic." *Down to Earth* 8/17 (January 31, 2000): 24-26.

Ananad, Rita. "Cleaning up the Frontyard." *Down to Earth* 3/19 (February 28, 1995): 23-24.

Banerjee, Proshanto. "A Fair Hearing." *Down to Earth* 11/5 (July 31, 2002): 50.

Banerjee, Tirtho. "Damnable Indispensability." *Down to Earth* 6/13 (November 30, 1997): 57.

Banerji, Rajat. "In the Line of Fire." *Down to Earth* 4/23 (April 30, 1996): 14-15.

__________. "What a Waste." *Down to Earth* 6/19 (September 30, 1997): 40-41.

Bharat Lal Seth, "Break the Odour," *Down to Earth* 18/21 (March 16-31, 2010): 9-10.

Bhat, A. N. "In Defense of Plastic." *Down to Earth* 10/24 (May 15, 2002): 2.

Borthakur, Ahir Bhairab. "Poser on Plastic." *Down to Earth* 10/12 (November 15, 2001): 24.

C. R. Neelakandan. "Jankeeyasamaram, N.G.O., Vidhesha Fund." *Mathrubhumi Azhchapathippu* 86/17 (December 7-13, 2008): 32-39.

Chandran, Civic. "Mahaswetha, Arundhathi Roy, Medha Padkar, Vandana Siva Ivar Keralathil karangunnath enthinu?" *Kalakaumudi* (June 22, 2008): 12-15.

Chikarmane, Poornima and Lakshmi Narayan. "Formalizing Livelihood: Case of Waste Pickers in Pune." *Economic and Political Weekly* 35/41 (October 7-13, 2000): 3639-3642.

Dastur, Mohazareen. "Unavoidable Reality: It's Time to Think Up Novel Ways to Manage Waste." *Down to Earth* 22/5 (July 16-31, 2013): 53.

Eloor, Purushan. "Chhenjunarunna Malineekarana Niyanthranama." *Mathrubhumi Azhchapathippu* 88/26 (September 5, 2010): 18-27.

Furedy, Christine. "Liquidation of Solid Waste." *Down to Earth* 4/14 (December 15, 1995): 52-53.

Greenhill. "Wealth from Waste." *Frontline* 10/19 (September 24, 1993): 75-77.

Hoering, Uwe. "Plasticky!" *Down to Earth* 8/13 (November 30, 1999): 57.

__________. "The Wasted Earth." *Down to Earth* 10/5 (April 15, 1994): 30-35.

Jamwal, Nidhi. "Reeds to the Issue." *Down to Earth* (July 31, 2001): 50-51.

__________. "Package Solutions." *Down to Earth* 11/14 (December 15, 2002): 24.

__________. "Swamped." *Down to Earth* 10/21 (March 31, 2002): 34-39.

Jayalal, J. S. "Vilappilsalayil Nirodhananga, Hartaal." *Janayugm* (February 14, 2012): 1.

Joseph, Sarah. "Nagarathinte Kuppathottikal." *Madhyamam Azhchapathippu* 734/15 (March 12, 2012): 25.

Kalra, Seema. "Wasteful Profits." *Down to Earth* 3/11 (October 31, 1994): 25-30.

Katakam, Anupama. "On the Scrap Heap." *Frontline* 18/15 (August 3, 2001): 89-92.

Kaur, Ravleen. "Partial Ban." *Down to Earth* 19/20 (March 1-15, 2011): 21.

Khushalini, Raksha and Rajat Banerji. "Should not Go Waste, This." *Down to Earth* 5/1 (May 31, 1996): 13-14.

Khanna, Anitha. "Garbage to Gold." *Down to Earth* 2/18 (February 15, 1994): 37-39.

Khandhari, Ruhi. "Plastic Shakeout." *Down to Earth* 18/15 (December 16-31, 2009): 24-25.

Malik, Iqbal. "Towards a Zero-Garbage City." *Manushi* 105 (March-April, 1998): 20-25.

Muthana, Ajay. "Rashtreeyam Azhukunna Malinyapuram." *Kalakaumudi* 38/47 (October 28, 2012): 4-11.

Menon, Ajit. "Decentralizing the Provision of Public Services: Exonera's Efforts at Garbage Collection in Madras." *Madras Institute of Development Studies* 23/1 (January, 1993): 22- 37.

Neelakandan, C. R. "Gramathil Kondupoyi Illathakkunna 'Prasnam'." *Mathrubhumi Azhchapathippu* 48/89 (February 11-17, 2012): 28-33.

Patel, Almitra H. "Enriching India's Soil." *Down to Earth* 10/12 (November 15, 2001): 52-53.

R. K. Srinivasan. "Urine is No Waste. "*Down to Earth* 14/11 (October 31, 2005): 46-47.

Rajesh, T. C. "Roshathinte Idimuzhakkam." *Kalakaumudi* 1903 (February 26, 212): 17-18.

Robin Murray. "Zero Waste." *Frontier* 42/14 (October 18-24, 2009): 14-15.

Schindler, Seth, Federicho Demaria and Shashi B. Pandit. "Delhi Waste Conflict." *Economic and Political Weekly* 47/42 (October 20, 2012): 18-21.

Sebastian, Marshal V. "Oru Gramam Sahichu, Ini Vayya." *Kalakaumudi* 1903 (February 26, 2012): 13.

Selvanayagam, Israel. "Apostle Judas! You Have a Special Appeal on Dialogue on Power and Authority." *Arasaradi Journal of Theological Reflection* 20 (July-December, 2007): 56-65.

Setharaman, S., C. A., Vijayachandran and N. Ramachandran. "Malinyam Malinyamkondu." *Mathrubhumi Azhchapathippu* 87/51 (28 February-6 March, 2010): 28-33.

Sethi, Aman. "Waste and Wealth." *Frontline* 23/7 (April 8-21, 2006): 86-88.

Shankar, M. "Keralam Oru Pannikoodu." *Samakalika Malayalam Varika* (October 25, 2002): 16-18.

Sharma, Monali. "Shear Waste." *Down to Earth* 10/21 (June 15, 2002): 24.

Snel, Marielle. "Development of Non- Government and Community-Based Organizations in Solid Waste Management Collection

Scheme." *The Indian Journal of Social Work* 62/4 (October, 2001): 618-638.

Sridhar, V. "Plastic Hazards." *Frontline* 19/11 (June 7, 2002): 36-39.

Srinivasan, Krithika. "Public, Private and Voluntary Agencies in Solid Waste Management: A Study in Chennai City. *Economic and Political Weekly* 41/22 (June 3, 2006): 2259-2267.

Suchithra, M. "Stench in My Backyard." *Down to Earth* 21/8 (September 1-15, 2012): 26-34.

Suchithra, M. and P. N. Venugopal."Malinyam Valarunnu Athirthikal Kadannum." *Mathrubhumi Azhchapathippu* 84/50 (February 11-17, 2007): 24-30.

Surjith, V., et al. "Chavarkoonayude Arikilninnum…" *Samakalika Malayalam Varika* 5/38 (February 1, 2002): 34.

Uganwa, Austin. "Filth is Food!" *Down to Earth* 5/6 (August 15, 1996): 22.

Venketeswaram, Sandhya. "Managing Waste: Ecological, Economic and Social Dimensions." *Economic and Plolitical Weekly* 29/56-46 (November 5-12, 1997): 2907-2920.

Victus, Solomon. "Jesus Approach to Proto- Zionism (The Zealot Movement)." *Arasaradi Journal of Theology* 23/1 & 2 (January-December, 2010): 1-11.

Venkataraman, S. "It's a Bad Synthetic World." *Down to Earth* 19/3 (June 16-30, 2010): 58.

5. TV Broadcasts

"Poabson Group Own Government Land in Thiruvananthapuram." *Reporter*, 7.00am, 12 January 2012.

6. Unpublished Manuscript Collections

Ramachandran, T.V. "Management of Municipal Solid Waste: Strategies." Manuscript of lecture delivered at Bangalore ECC Seminar on Soild Waste Management, 25 September 2012.

"Malinya Samskaranam –Prasnangalum Sadhyathakalum: Janakeeya Samvadam." Thiruvananthapuram Corporation, 2013.

C. Webliography

http://www.censusindia.gov.in (17 July 2013).

http://www.censusindia.gov.in/PopulationFinder/View_Village_Population.aspx?pcaid=506071&category=VILLAGE (17 July 2013).

http://www.corporationoftrivandrum.in (17 July 2013).

http://www.keralagov.in (17 July 2013).

H. Patel, Almitra. "Urban Solid Waste Management: Progress and Prospects for Social, Technical and Policy Improvement." http://www.almitrapatel.com (19 August 2013).

Abdulla, M. P. "Trends, Causes and Consequences of Consumerism in Kerala" (2008).

Department of Economics, University of Calicut. http://www.shodhganga.inflibnet.ac.in/handle/10603/594 (30 September 2013).

"Government to Shift Garbage Processing plant from Vilappilsala." http://www.keralacm.gov.in (21 December 2011).

K. P. Thrivikramji. "Kerala's Baby Steps Toward Sanitation: The Vilappilsala Plant." http://www.trivikramji.com (12 February 2012).

Cooke, Robert. "The Caste System of India." *Trinicenter Special.* http://www.raceandhistory.com/historicalviews/casteindia.htm (18 November 2013).

"Indian Plasic Industry." http://www.india-exports.com/plastic.html (10 March 2014).

"Pollution Near Kureepuzha Alarming: Study." *The Hindu* (13 August 2011). http://www.thehindu.com/todays-paper/tp-national/tp-kerala/pollution-near-kureepuzha-alarming-study/article2352864.ece (5 March 2014).

Appendix I

Questionnaire

I am .... doing MTh in Social Analysis at .... As part of my studies I am researching on 'Vilappilsala Janakeeya Samithy and Solid Waste Disposal in Trivandrum', dealing with the study of the waste management issues in Trivandrum and the plight of the people of Vilappilsala, which has been selected by the city Corporation for the disposal of waste and the impact of the plant on the life of the villagers. It would be of great help to my research if you could kindly answer the questions below. Your responses will be strictly kept confidential.

NB: Please give a tick mark (√) in the columns wherever necessary. You are free to tick more than one answer wherever necessary. Thank you.

Sincerely,

Name:

Seminary:

Place:

Date:

....

Gender : Male ☐ Female ☐

Age Group : a) Below 15 b) 15-20
c) 21-30 d) 31-40
e) 41-50 f) 51-60
g) 61-70 h) Above 70

Occupation : Daily Wage labour ☐ Agriculture ☐
Government ☐ Private ☐ Others ☐

Place : ....

Distance from the plant: .... m/km

....

1. Why did you participate in the struggle?
   a) as it directly affects them ☐
   b) as a common problem ☐
   c) at the compulsion of protestors ☐
   d) of all reasons ☐
   e) none of the above ☐
2. How often the stench created problems to the villagers?
   a) always ☐
   b) during the stirring of garbage ☐
   c) at the transportation of garbage trucks ☐
   d) none of the above ☐
3. What are the health problems you have experienced when the plant was operational?
   i) Breathing Uneasiness
      a) always ☐
      b) occasional ☐
      c) while stirring the waste ☐
      d) transportation of the waste ☐
      e) can't say ☐
   ii) Itching
      a) always ☐ b) occasional ☐ c) no itching ☐

iii) Skin disease

a) always ☐ b) occasional ☐ c) no skin disease ☐

iv) Other problems as stray dogs, rodents, flies and birds

a) always ☐ b) occasional ☐ c) no skin disease ☐

v) Do you still have the same problem?

a) Yes ☐ b) No ☐

4. What kind of water you are using for domestic purpose and washing cattle?

a) well ☐ b) rivulet ☐ c) both ☐
d) pipe ☐ e) all ☐

5. Which water was more polluted?

a) well ☐ b) rivulet ☐ c) both ☐
d) pipe ☐ e) all ☐

6. Do your son's/daughter's/ brother's/ sisters/ relatives marriage proposal fail because of the plant?

a) Yes ☐ b) No ☐ c) Can't say ☐

7. How did the village local community respond to the workers in the plant?

a) Threatened and excluded them from public functions ☐
b) Advised them to do other jobs ☐
c) Both ☐ a) and b) ☐ c) Behaved as usual ☐
d) Comforted them and advised them to accept their plight ☐
e) None of the above ☐

8. Who were larger in number to participate in the struggle?

a) Men ☐ b) Women ☐
c) Equally ☐ d) Can't say ☐

9. Have you sold your land at the location due to the garbage treatment plant?

a) Yes ☐ b) No ☐

10. Have you lost your work because of the plant?
    a) Yes ☐ b) No ☐ c) Can't say ☐
11. How did the police force behave?
    a) Good ☐ b) Bad ☐ c) Don't know ☐
12. Who made violence in the struggle?
    a) Police ☐ b) Villagers ☐
    c) Outsiders ☐ d) All of them
13. Do you believe in any political parties?
    a) Yes ☐ b) No ☐ c) Can't say ☐
14. Did the print and visual media give importance to your issue?
    a) Yes ☐ b) No ☐
15. Whose was the success of the struggle?
    a) People ☐
    b) Vilappilsala Janakeeya Samithy ☐
    c) Samyuktha Samara Samithy ☐
    d) Panchayat ☐
    e) None of the above ☐
16. Is it possible to have a world without waste?
    a) Yes ☐ b) No ☐ c) Can't say ☐
17. Which is the suitable method for waste disposal?
    a) compost making ☐ b) burning ☐
    c) burying ☐ d) throwing out ☐
    e) source level treatment f) mini plants ☐
    g) all are good ☐
18. What you are doing with your own household waste?
    a) source level treatment ☐ b) compost making ☐
    c) burying ☐ d) burning especially plastic ☐
    e) throwing out ☐ f) doing all the above ☐
19. Do you know burning plastic result in carcinogenic disease?
    a) Yes b) No

20. What should the Corporation do with the waste?
    a) Find other places for waste disposal ☐
    b) treat waste with new machines ☐
    c) dispose waste in Corporation's property ☐
    d) whatever be done, no garbage should be brought to Vilappilsala ☐
    e) none of the above ☐
21. Do you participate in the struggle if the factory reopens and functions without making trouble?
    a) Yes ☐ b) No ☐ c) Can't say ☐
22. Did your church leaders especially pastors give support and participate/ in the struggle?
    a) Yes ☐ b) No ☐ c) Can't say ☐

Appendix II

The open prison is situated in Nettukaltheri, 28 km away from the city which is near Neyyar Dam. If implemented, pollution from the plant will affect the reservoir, the Kalipara drinking water project, providing water to three panchayats Kallikadu, Kuttichal and Poovachal and around 400 inmates of the open prison ("Nettukaltheri Thuranna Jail Vilappilsalayakkaruthu," *Kerala Kaumudi* (Thiruvananthapuram), 3 January 2012, 1.).

The tea estate is located in Bonacaud, 35km away from the city. The government selected this area along with other ecologically sensitive places such as Shamgili, Idinjar, Mankayam, Pampuchattamannu and Arippa in Palode and Kulathupuzha forest ranges (S. T. Biju, "Malinya Bhoomikku Pattikayayi," *Kerala Kaumudi* (Thiruvananthapuram), 3 January 2012, 2.).

The government has identified 20 abandoned granite quarries to dump waste. The government proposed that it would take adequate measures which include draining the water into adjacent quarries, cement filling of the fissures, laying of clay liner, spreading of polythene sheets of 1.5 mm thickness, drainage layer (coarse aggregate) followed by perforated PVC pipes, preparation for subsequent layers including metal, waste, mud and another layer of polythene sheets to be finished in phases (Denis Marcus Mathew, "Mission Swears by Quarry Option," *The Hindu* (Thiruvanathapuram), 15 October 2012, 3.). This is to prevent leachate flow ("Plan to Revive the Quarry Option," *The Hindu* (Thiruvanathapuram), 2 October 2012, 3.). In places like Chenkottukonam and Kallidichavila, which was used as a drinking water source, the Corporation counselors themselves came with protest ("Defiant Protestors Put Government in a Dither," *The Hindu* (Thiruvanathapuram), 12 October 2012, 3.). These plans were also deserted as the people began to protest from the initial stage itself ("Garbage Quarries in Two Days," *The Hindu* (Thiruvanathapuram), 11 October 2012, 3.).

The railway has identified 31 places where waste can be used for constructing railway platform. In Kochuveli, the government wanted to dump 400 loads of waste, but could only transport 84 loads followed by people's protest ("Chavarneekam: Asayakuzhappam Thudarunnu," *Kerala Kaumudi* (Thiruvananthapuram), 27 June 2012, 3.). The transportation waste to Murukkumpuzha railway platform was stopped after the intervention of the people and the police ("Nattukar Lorrie Thadanju: 17 Per Arrestil," *Kerala Kaumudi* (Thiruvananthapuram), 21 June 2012, 3.). The police in Pothencode police station seized bulldozers used to collect soil to the platform ("J.C.B. Pidicheduthathu Poleesinu Pulivalayi," *Kerala Kaumudi* (Thiruvananthapuram), 18 June 2012, 3.). Another proposal was to use the waste for making railway platform in Parassala ("Parassala Platfrom Nirmanathinu Malinyam," *Malayala Manorama* (Thiruvananthapuram), 15 August 2012, 8.). This plan had a premature end ("Malinyam Parassalayilekku Neekkilla; Nagaram Narunnu," *Malayala Manorama* (Thiruvananthapuram), 11 September 2012, 2.).

The proposal for land filling was to be done in Veyiloor, 25 km away from the city, where there is an abandoned clay mine which is 50 ft deep and 14 acre area. In order to control the people's protest the government promised that the land filled area would be used to upgrade the government high school to higher secondary school ("Veyiloor Swapnavum Palunnu; Sarkar Vishamavrithathil," *Kerala Kaumudi* (Thiruvananthapuram), 1 August 2012, 3.). The government withdrew its proposal following strong resistance from Azhoor and Mangalapuram panchayats ("Nagaramalinyam Njangalkku Venda; School Paniyan Anchekkar Tharu," *Malayala Manorama* (Thiruvananthapuram), 1 August 2012, 13.).

The ban on throwing garbage was done in the context of the spread of epidemics in the city. According to the order, those who dump waste on the road side will be arrested on non bailable conditions ("Malinyam Valicheriyunnavar Sookshikkuka Pidiyilakum Jamyamilla Vakuppil," *Kerala Kaumudi* (Thiruvananthapuram), 13 June 2012, 3.). Another decision was to unauthorized butcheries, street vendors to be controlled and petty shops could open only up to a limited time ("Malinyamerinjal Ini Jailinakathu," *Malayala Manorama* (Thiruvananthapuram), 5 June 2012, 1.). They constituted special squad for ensuring that the order was implemented ("Malinyam Valicheriyalle, Squadirnagi..." *Kerala Kaumudi* (Thiruvananthapuram) 12 June 2012, 3.).

Appendix III

The State government has allotted Rs. 5.7 crore to Corporation for the project through Swuchitva Mission, a Governmental body ("Uravidathil Malinya Samskaranam: Nagara Sabha Paddhathi Izhayunnu," *Malayala Manorama* (Thiruvananthapuram), 5 April 2012, 7.). This amount is very meagre to install pipe compost in a city whose population is 10 lakh ("Pipe Compost Paddhathi Nadathipil Veezhcha: Corporation Secretariye Vilichuvaruthan Nirddesam," *Malayala Manorama* (Thiruvananthapuram), 12 June 2012, 2.).

The mobile incinerator has the capacity to burn 0.49 tonne waste per hour ("Incinerator to be Shifted to Eenchakkal on Monday," *The Hindu* (Thiruvananthapuram), 14 January 2013, 3.). It can be operated for only eight hours a day and consumes 50-80 liters of diesel ("Mobile Incinerator's Record: 40 tonnes of garbage in 45 Hours," *The Hindu* (Thiruvananthapuram), 15 October 2012, 3.). The limitation is that it cannot burn around 200 tonnes of waste produced in the city and was shut down following the government's dissatisfaction over its performance and the government's non-payment of Rs. 34 lakhs to its manufacturer, Chintan Sales, Ahammadabad ("Mobile Incinerator was Shut Down," *The Hindu* (Thiruvananthapuram), 12 March 2013, 3.). Later it was shifted to Malappuram (Interview with Santhosh, JAT, Thiruvananthapuram Corporation, 13 December 2013.).

This is the first of the four plants to be constructed ("Consensus Reached on Chalai Plant: Ministers," *The Hindu* (Thiruvananthapuram), 24 January 2013, 3.). The others are those at Kazhakoottam, Nemom and Vattiyoorkavu ("Sites Identified for Waste Treatment Plants," *The Hindu* (Thiruvananthapuram), 1 February 2013, 3.). It is supposed to treat up to 35 tonnes of garbage a day and produce 3.5 MW electricity ("How the Chalai Garbage Plant was Gift-wrapped," *The Hindu* (Thiruvananthapuram), 25 January 2013, 3.). It is estimated that the total cost of the plant would be Rs.65 crore and would be run by the US based Lora Group for 20 years ("Chala Garbage Plant Likely by March," *The Hindu* (Thiruvananthapuram), 15 November 2012, 3.).

Appendix IV

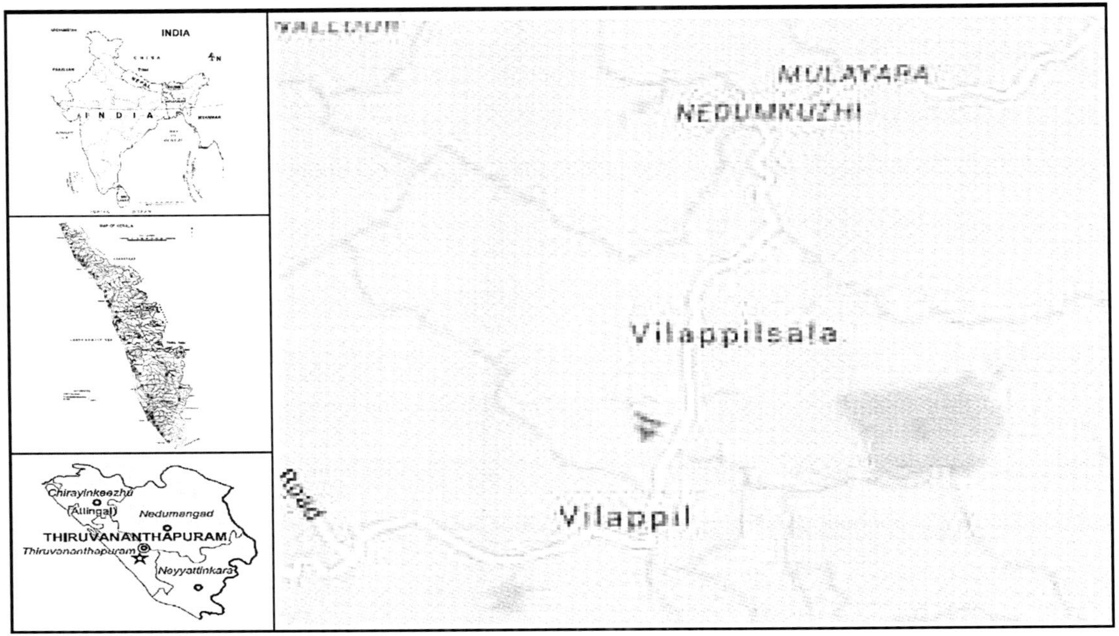

Location of the Study Area
(Maps not to be scaled)